The Anxiety Toolkit

Self-help, Volume 6

Timothy Scott Phillips

Published by Arcane Horizons Publishing, 2024.

While every precaution has been taken in the preparation of this book, the publisher assumes no responsibility for errors or omissions, or for damages resulting from the use of the information contained herein.

THE ANXIETY TOOLKIT

First edition. December 1, 2024.

Copyright © 2024 Timothy Scott Phillips.

ISBN: 979-8230566373

Written by Timothy Scott Phillips.

Table of Contents

The Anxiety Toolkit (Self-help, #6) 1

Chapter 1: Understanding Anxiety 7

Chapter 2: Recognizing Phobias 14

Chapter 3: The Anxiety-Phobia Connection 27

Chapter 4: Self-Assessment and Diagnosis 36

Chapter 5: Cognitive-Behavioral Techniques 49

Chapter 6: Exposure Therapy 61

Chapter 7: Mindfulness and Relaxation Techniques 73

Chapter 8: Lifestyle Changes for Anxiety Management 86

Chapter 9: Medication and Alternative Therapies 98

Chapter 10: Support Systems and Social Connections 110

Chapter 11: Coping Strategies for Daily Life 122

Chapter 12: Long-Term Strategies for Resilience 134

Chapter 13: Helping Others with Anxiety and Phobias 143

Chapter 14: Success Stories and Inspirational Journeys 152

Chapter 15: Resources and Further Reading 161

To everyone who has ever felt trapped by their fears,

This book is for you.

May it be a light in your darkest moments,

a guide when the path seems uncertain,

and a reminder that courage is not the absence of fear,

but the determination to move forward despite it.

To the loved ones who stand by, offering patience and hope,

your support is a lifeline.

Together, we rise above.

Introduction

Overview of Anxiety and Phobias

Definition and Differences Between Anxiety and Phobias

ANXIETY AND PHOBIAS, though often used interchangeably in casual conversation, represent distinct phenomena within the realm of mental health. Understanding the nuances between these two terms is essential for anyone seeking to manage their symptoms effectively and lead a fulfilling life.

Anxiety

Anxiety is a general term for several disorders that cause nervousness, fear, apprehension, and worrying. It can affect how we feel and behave and can manifest real physical symptoms. Mild anxiety is vague and unsettling, while severe anxiety can be extremely debilitating, having a serious impact on daily life.

Common symptoms of anxiety include:

- Increased heart rate

- Rapid breathing

- Restlessness

- Trouble concentrating

- Difficulty falling asleep

Anxiety can be classified into various types, including generalized anxiety disorder (GAD), social anxiety disorder, panic disorder, and specific phobias. Generalized anxiety disorder, for example, is characterized by excessive, uncontrollable worry about everyday things, often accompanied by physical symptoms such as fatigue, muscle tension, and headaches.

Phobias

Phobias, on the other hand, are a type of anxiety disorder characterized by an intense, irrational fear of specific objects, situations, or activities. The fear is so severe that it can cause individuals to avoid the feared object or situation entirely, often leading to significant impairment in daily functioning.

There are three main types of phobias:

1. Specific Phobias: These involve an irrational fear of a specific object or situation, such as heights (acrophobia), spiders (arachnophobia), or flying (aviophobia).

2. Social Phobia (Social Anxiety Disorder): This involves a significant fear of social situations where one might be embarrassed, judged, or scrutinized by others.

3. Agoraphobia: This involves a fear of places or situations where escape might be difficult, or help unavailable, particularly in the event of a panic attack. It often leads to the avoidance of situations such as crowded places, public transportation, or being alone outside the home.

Prevalence and Impact on Daily Life

ANXIETY AND PHOBIAS are remarkably common, affecting millions of people worldwide. According to the World Health Organization (WHO), approximately 264 million people globally suffer from anxiety disorders, making them one of the most prevalent mental health conditions.

Anxiety Disorders

ANXIETY DISORDERS ARE the most common mental illness in the United States, affecting 40 million adults aged 18 and older, which is about 18.1% of the population each year. Despite their prevalence, anxiety disorders are highly treatable, yet only about 36.9% of those suffering receive treatment. This gap in treatment highlights the importance of education, awareness, and accessibility to mental health resources.

The impact of anxiety disorders on daily life can be profound. Individuals may experience difficulty in maintaining personal relationships, performing at work or school, and participating in social activities. Chronic anxiety can also lead to physical health problems, such as heart disease, gastrointestinal issues, and a weakened immune system.

Phobias

Phobias, while often less discussed, are also widespread. Specific phobias affect approximately 19 million American adults, or 8.7% of the U.S. population. Social anxiety disorder affects about 15 million adults, and agoraphobia affects approximately 1.8 million adults.

The impact of phobias on daily life can be equally debilitating. For instance, someone with a severe fear of flying might avoid traveling altogether, limiting both personal and professional opportunities. Similarly, a person with social phobia may avoid social gatherings, hindering their ability to form and maintain relationships.

Purpose and Goals of the Book

THE PURPOSE OF THIS book is to provide a comprehensive, practical guide for managing anxiety and phobias. By understanding the underlying mechanisms of these conditions and exploring a variety of effective tools and techniques, readers can develop personalized strategies to reduce their symptoms and improve their quality of life.

Education and Awareness

ONE OF THE PRIMARY goals of this book is to educate readers about anxiety and phobias. Understanding the biological, psychological, and environmental factors that contribute to these conditions can empower individuals to take control of their mental health. Knowledge is a powerful tool, and by demystifying anxiety and phobias, this book aims to reduce the stigma often associated with these disorders.

Practical Tools and Techniques

THIS BOOK PROVIDES a toolkit of evidence-based strategies for managing anxiety and phobias. From cognitive-behavioral techniques and exposure therapy to mindfulness practices and lifestyle changes, readers will have access to a wide range of approaches that can be tailored to their unique needs and preferences. Each chapter will include practical exercises, real-life examples, and step-by-step guides to help readers implement these strategies effectively.

Building Resilience and Long-Term Strategies

IN ADDITION TO PROVIDING immediate relief, this book emphasizes the importance of building emotional resilience and developing long-term strategies for managing anxiety and phobias. By cultivating a growth mindset, developing healthy coping mechanisms, and maintaining a balanced lifestyle, readers can enhance their ability to navigate life's challenges and prevent relapse.

Support and Community

FINALLY, THIS BOOK highlights the importance of support systems and social connections in the journey towards managing anxiety and phobias. Whether it's family, friends, support groups, or professional help, having a strong support network can make a significant difference in one's recovery process. This book will provide resources and guidance on how to build and maintain these connections.

Structure of the Book

THE STRUCTURE OF THIS book is designed to guide readers through a comprehensive journey of understanding and managing anxiety and phobias. Each chapter builds on the previous one, providing a logical progression from education and awareness to practical tools and long-term strategies.

THE ANXIETY TOOLKIT

Chapter Summaries

1. UNDERSTANDING ANXIETY: This chapter delves into the biological and psychological explanations of anxiety, common symptoms, and the different types of anxiety disorders.

2. Recognizing Phobias: Readers will learn about the various types of phobias, their causes, and how they develop and manifest.

3. The Anxiety-Phobia Connection: This chapter explores how anxiety and phobias interact, using case studies to illustrate the vicious cycle of fear and avoidance.

4. Self-Assessment and Diagnosis: Tools and questionnaires for identifying triggers and understanding one's diagnosis are provided.

5. Cognitive-Behavioral Techniques: Practical exercises for challenging negative thoughts and changing thought patterns are discussed.

6. Exposure Therapy: A step-by-step guide to facing fears gradually through exposure therapy.

7. Mindfulness and Relaxation Techniques: Readers will learn about mindfulness, breathing exercises, and progressive muscle relaxation.

8. Lifestyle Changes for Anxiety Management: The impact of diet, exercise, sleep, and self-care on anxiety management is covered.

9. Medication and Alternative Therapies: An overview of medications and alternative therapies for anxiety and phobias.

10. Support Systems and Social Connections: Guidance on building a support network and the role of family and friends in recovery.

11. Coping Strategies for Daily Life: Practical tips for handling anxiety in various situations and creating an anxiety management plan.

12. Long-Term Strategies for Resilience: Strategies for building emotional resilience, maintaining progress, and preventing relapse.

13. Helping Others with Anxiety and Phobias: How to recognize anxiety and phobias in others and offer effective support.

14. Success Stories and Inspirational Journeys: Real-life stories of individuals overcoming anxiety and phobias, along with interviews and testimonials.

15. Resources and Further Reading: Recommended books, websites, organizations, online courses, and workshops for ongoing self-improvement and support.

Conclusion

The conclusion will recap the key points and strategies discussed throughout the book, offering final thoughts and encouragement to readers. It will emphasize the importance of persistence, self-compassion, and the ongoing journey towards managing anxiety and phobias.

By the end of this book, readers will have a deep understanding of anxiety and phobias, along with a comprehensive toolkit of practical strategies to manage their symptoms and improve their overall well-being. This journey is not about achieving perfection but about making steady progress towards a more balanced, fulfilling life.

Chapter 1: Understanding Anxiety

What is Anxiety?

Anxiety is a complex and multifaceted condition that affects millions of people worldwide. It is characterized by feelings of worry, nervousness, or fear that are strong enough to interfere with one's daily activities. Understanding anxiety requires an exploration of its biological and psychological underpinnings, its common symptoms, the various types of anxiety disorders, and the role of genetics and environmental factors.

Biological and Psychological Explanations

Biological Explanations

FROM A BIOLOGICAL PERSPECTIVE, anxiety is often understood in terms of the brain's chemistry and the functioning of the nervous system. The human brain is an incredibly complex organ, and its proper functioning relies on the delicate balance of neurotransmitters, which are chemicals that transmit signals between nerve cells. Two of the most important neurotransmitters involved in anxiety are serotonin and gamma-aminobutyric acid (GABA).

1. Serotonin: Often referred to as the "feel-good" neurotransmitter, serotonin plays a key role in mood regulation. Low levels of serotonin have been linked to anxiety and depression. Medications that increase serotonin levels, such as selective serotonin reuptake inhibitors (SSRIs), are commonly used to treat anxiety disorders.

2. GABA: GABA is an inhibitory neurotransmitter that helps to calm the nervous system. It works by reducing the activity of neurons, making it less likely that they will fire. Low levels of GABA can result in an overactive brain, leading to heightened anxiety. Benzodiazepines, a class of drugs used to treat anxiety, work by enhancing the effects of GABA.

Additionally, the body's fight-or-flight response plays a crucial role in anxiety. This response is a survival mechanism that prepares the body to either confront or flee from a perceived threat. When the brain perceives a danger, the hypothalamus signals the adrenal glands to release adrenaline and cortisol, hormones that increase heart rate, blood pressure, and blood sugar levels, providing the energy needed for quick action. In people with anxiety disorders, this fight-or-flight response may be triggered inappropriately or excessively, even in the absence of real danger.

Psychological Explanations

PSYCHOLOGICAL THEORIES of anxiety focus on the ways in which thoughts, beliefs, and behaviors contribute to the development and maintenance of anxiety disorders. Some of the most influential psychological explanations include:

1. Cognitive Theories: These theories suggest that anxiety arises from maladaptive thought patterns and cognitive distortions. For example, individuals with anxiety may have a tendency to overestimate the likelihood of negative events occurring or to catastrophize, imagining the worst possible outcomes. Cognitive-behavioral therapy (CBT), a widely used treatment for anxiety, focuses on identifying and challenging these distorted thought patterns.

2. Behavioral Theories: Behavioral theories emphasize the role of learned behaviors in the development of anxiety. Classical conditioning, a process in which a neutral stimulus becomes associated with a fearful response, can lead to the development of specific phobias. For example, if a person is bitten by a dog, they may develop a fear of all dogs. Operant conditioning, which involves the reinforcement of behaviors, can also play a role. Avoidance behaviors, which are negatively reinforced by the reduction of anxiety, can maintain and exacerbate anxiety disorders.

3. Psychodynamic Theories: These theories, rooted in the work of Sigmund Freud, propose that anxiety is the result of unconscious conflicts and unresolved emotional issues. According to this perspective, anxiety arises when

repressed feelings, thoughts, or memories threaten to enter conscious awareness. Psychodynamic therapy aims to uncover and resolve these underlying conflicts.

Common Symptoms and Types of Anxiety Disorders

ANXIETY CAN MANIFEST in a variety of ways, and the symptoms can range from mild to severe. Common symptoms of anxiety include:

- Excessive worry or fear

- Restlessness or feeling on edge

- Irritability

- Difficulty concentrating

- Muscle tension

- Sleep disturbances

- Rapid heart rate

- Shortness of breath

- Sweating

- Trembling or shaking

- Gastrointestinal issues (e.g., nausea, diarrhea)

The Diagnostic and Statistical Manual of Mental Disorders, Fifth Edition (DSM-5), classifies anxiety disorders into several distinct categories, each with its own specific criteria. The most common types of anxiety disorders include:

1. Generalized Anxiety Disorder (GAD): GAD is characterized by persistent and excessive worry about a variety of everyday situations. Individuals with GAD often find it difficult to control their worry, and they may experience physical symptoms such as fatigue, muscle tension, and headaches. The worry

in GAD is often disproportionate to the actual likelihood or impact of the feared events.

2. Panic Disorder: Panic disorder involves recurrent and unexpected panic attacks, which are sudden episodes of intense fear that peak within minutes. Symptoms of a panic attack can include palpitations, sweating, trembling, shortness of breath, chest pain, dizziness, and a fear of losing control or dying. People with panic disorder often develop a fear of future attacks and may avoid situations where they fear an attack might occur.

3. Social Anxiety Disorder (Social Phobia): Social anxiety disorder is characterized by an intense fear of social situations in which one might be scrutinized or judged by others. This fear can lead to avoidance of social interactions, which can significantly impair a person's ability to function in daily life. Common situations that trigger social anxiety include public speaking, meeting new people, and eating in public.

4. Specific Phobias: Specific phobias involve an irrational and excessive fear of a specific object, situation, or activity. Common phobias include fears of animals (e.g., spiders, snakes), natural environments (e.g., heights, storms), blood-injection-injury (e.g., needles, medical procedures), and situational phobias (e.g., flying, elevators). The fear experienced in specific phobias is often disproportionate to the actual danger posed by the object or situation.

5. Agoraphobia: Agoraphobia involves a fear of situations where escape might be difficult or help might not be available in the event of a panic attack or other incapacitating symptoms. People with agoraphobia may avoid places such as crowded areas, public transportation, or being alone outside their home. In severe cases, agoraphobia can lead to complete avoidance of leaving home.

6. Obsessive-Compulsive Disorder (OCD): While OCD is classified separately from anxiety disorders in the DSM-5, it is closely related and often involves significant anxiety. OCD is characterized by the presence of obsessions (intrusive, unwanted thoughts) and compulsions (repetitive behaviors or mental acts performed to reduce anxiety). Common obsessions include fears of

contamination, harm, or making mistakes, while common compulsions include washing, checking, and counting.

The Role of Genetics and Environment

THE DEVELOPMENT OF anxiety disorders is influenced by a combination of genetic and environmental factors. Understanding the interplay between these factors can help to explain why some individuals are more susceptible to anxiety than others.

Genetic Factors

RESEARCH HAS SHOWN that anxiety disorders tend to run in families, suggesting a genetic component. Twin studies have provided evidence for the heritability of anxiety disorders, with estimates ranging from 30% to 50%. Specific genes that influence the regulation of neurotransmitters, such as serotonin and GABA, have been implicated in the development of anxiety.

One of the most well-studied genes in relation to anxiety is the serotonin transporter gene (SLC6A4). Variations in this gene can affect the reuptake of serotonin in the brain, influencing mood and anxiety levels. Individuals with a particular variant of this gene, known as the short allele, have been found to have an increased risk of developing anxiety disorders, particularly when exposed to stressful life events.

Another gene of interest is the gene encoding for the enzyme catechol-O-methyltransferase (COMT), which is involved in the breakdown of dopamine. Variations in this gene have been associated with differences in anxiety sensitivity and the regulation of the stress response.

Environmental Factors

WHILE GENETICS PLAY a significant role in the development of anxiety disorders, environmental factors are also crucial. Some of the key environmental factors that can contribute to anxiety include:

1. Childhood Adversity: Traumatic experiences in childhood, such as abuse, neglect, or the loss of a parent, can increase the risk of developing anxiety disorders later in life. These adverse experiences can disrupt the development of the brain's stress response systems, making individuals more vulnerable to anxiety.

2. Parenting Styles: Overprotective or controlling parenting styles have been linked to higher levels of anxiety in children. Conversely, supportive and nurturing parenting can promote resilience and reduce the risk of anxiety disorders.

3. Life Stressors: Significant life changes or stressors, such as the loss of a loved one, divorce, job loss, or financial difficulties, can trigger the onset of anxiety disorders. Chronic stress, in particular, can have a cumulative effect, increasing the likelihood of developing anxiety.

4. Social Environment: The social environment, including relationships with family, friends, and peers, can influence anxiety levels. Social support can act as a protective factor, while social isolation or negative social interactions can exacerbate anxiety.

5. Cultural Factors: Cultural beliefs and norms can also play a role in the development and expression of anxiety. For example, in some cultures, expressing emotions may be discouraged, leading to increased internalization of anxiety. Additionally, cultural differences in the perception and interpretation of stressors can impact the prevalence and manifestation of anxiety disorders.

Interaction of Genetics and Environment

THE INTERACTION BETWEEN genetic and environmental factors is complex, and the development of anxiety disorders is often the result of a combination of both. The diathesis-stress model is a widely accepted framework for understanding this interaction. According to this model, individuals with a genetic predisposition (diathesis) for anxiety are more likely to develop an anxiety disorder when exposed to significant stressors.

For example, a person with a family history of anxiety may have a genetic vulnerability to the disorder. If this individual experiences a major life stressor, such as the death of a loved one or a traumatic event, the combination of genetic vulnerability and environmental stress can trigger the onset of an anxiety disorder.

Conclusion

Anxiety is a multifaceted condition influenced by a complex interplay of biological, psychological, genetic, and environmental factors. By understanding the underlying mechanisms of anxiety, individuals can gain insight into their experiences and develop effective strategies for managing their symptoms.

In the chapters that follow, we will explore various tools and techniques for managing anxiety, including cognitive-behavioral therapy, mindfulness practices, lifestyle changes, and more. By equipping yourself with a comprehensive toolkit of strategies, you can take control of your anxiety and work towards a more balanced and fulfilling life.

Remember, managing anxiety is a journey, and progress may be gradual. It's important to be patient with yourself and to seek support when needed. With the right knowledge and resources, you can develop the resilience and skills needed to navigate the challenges of anxiety and lead a life that is not defined by fear.

Chapter 2: Recognizing Phobias

Types of Phobias

Phobias are a type of anxiety disorder characterized by an excessive, irrational fear of specific objects, situations, or activities. While everyone experiences fear at times, phobias go beyond normal fear reactions and can significantly interfere with daily life. This chapter delves into the different types of phobias, their causes and risk factors, and how they develop and manifest.

Specific Phobias

SPECIFIC PHOBIAS INVOLVE an intense fear of a particular object or situation that is generally disproportionate to the actual danger posed. These phobias are common and can be categorized into several subtypes based on the nature of the feared object or situation:

1. Animal Phobias: These are fears related to animals or insects. Common examples include:

- **Arachnophobia**: Fear of spiders

- **Ophidiophobia**: Fear of snakes

- **Cynophobia**: Fear of dogs

2. Natural Environment Phobias: These involve fears of natural occurrences or environments. Common examples include:

- **Acrophobia**: Fear of heights

- **Astraphobia**: Fear of thunder and lightning

- **Hydrophobia**: Fear of water

3. Blood-Injection-Injury Phobias: These phobias are related to medical procedures or the sight of blood. Common examples include:

- **Trypanophobia**: Fear of needles or injections

- **Hemophobia**: Fear of blood

- **Dentophobia**: Fear of dentists or dental procedures

4. Situational Phobias: These involve fears of specific situations. Common examples include:

- **Claustrophobia**: Fear of confined spaces

- **Aviophobia**: Fear of flying

- **Elevatophobia**: Fear of elevators

5. Other Phobias: These include less common fears that do not fall into the above categories. Examples include:

- **Emetophobia**: Fear of vomiting

- **Nomophobia**: Fear of being without a mobile phone

Specific phobias can cause significant distress and avoidance behaviors. For instance, someone with a severe fear of dogs may avoid parks, neighborhoods, or even social gatherings where dogs might be present.

Social Phobia (Social Anxiety Disorder)

SOCIAL PHOBIA, ALSO known as social anxiety disorder, involves an intense fear of social situations where one might be judged, embarrassed, or scrutinized by others. This fear can lead to significant avoidance behaviors and impair one's ability to function in social or professional settings. Key aspects of social phobia include:

1. Performance Situations: Fear of performing in front of others, such as public speaking, giving presentations, or performing on stage. Individuals may worry about making mistakes, being criticized, or being the center of attention.

2. Social Interactions: Fear of interacting with others, particularly strangers or authority figures. This can include fears of initiating conversations, making eye contact, or participating in group activities.

3. Observation Situations: Fear of being observed by others, such as eating in public, using public restrooms, or writing in front of others.

Social phobia often begins in adolescence or early adulthood and can persist throughout life if not addressed. It can lead to significant impairment in personal, academic, and professional domains, as individuals may avoid opportunities that involve social interaction or performance.

Agoraphobia

Agoraphobia involves a fear of situations where escape might be difficult or help might not be available in the event of a panic attack or other incapacitating symptoms. This fear can lead to avoidance of a wide range of situations, including:

1. Public Transportation: Fear of using buses, trains, subways, or airplanes. Individuals may worry about being trapped or unable to escape if they experience anxiety or a panic attack.

2. Open Spaces: Fear of being in open or crowded places, such as shopping malls, markets, or parking lots. The vastness or crowd density can trigger feelings of vulnerability and fear.

3. Enclosed Spaces: Fear of being in confined spaces, such as elevators, movie theaters, or small rooms. The limited ability to leave these spaces can exacerbate anxiety.

4. Being Away from Home: Fear of being far from home or in unfamiliar places. Individuals may feel a strong need to stay close to home where they feel safe and in control.

Agoraphobia often develops in conjunction with panic disorder, as individuals may begin to fear the situations in which they have previously experienced panic attacks. This fear can lead to severe avoidance behaviors and significant impairment in daily functioning, as individuals may become increasingly restricted in their activities and environment.

Causes and Risk Factors

PHOBIAS CAN DEVELOP for a variety of reasons, and their onset is typically influenced by a combination of genetic, environmental, and psychological factors. Understanding these causes and risk factors can provide insight into why some individuals develop phobias while others do not.

Genetic Factors

GENETIC PREDISPOSITION plays a significant role in the development of phobias. Studies have shown that phobias can run in families, suggesting a hereditary component. Twin studies have demonstrated that identical twins are more likely to share specific phobias compared to fraternal twins, indicating a genetic influence.

Specific genes related to the regulation of neurotransmitters, such as serotonin and dopamine, have been implicated in the development of phobias. Variations in these genes can affect how the brain processes fear and anxiety, making some individuals more susceptible to developing phobias.

Environmental Factors

ENVIRONMENTAL FACTORS, particularly during childhood, can significantly contribute to the development of phobias. Some key environmental factors include:

1. Traumatic Experiences: A single traumatic event, such as being bitten by a dog or experiencing a natural disaster, can lead to the development of a phobia. The intense fear and distress associated with the event can create a lasting fear response.

2. Parental Influence: Parents play a crucial role in shaping their children's behavior and responses to fear. Overprotective or anxious parenting styles can

model fearful behaviors and reinforce avoidance. Conversely, parents who encourage exploration and model coping strategies can help mitigate the development of phobias.

3. Observational Learning: Phobias can also develop through observational learning, where individuals learn to fear certain objects or situations by observing others' fearful reactions. For example, a child who sees a parent react fearfully to spiders may develop a fear of spiders themselves.

4. Cultural Factors: Cultural beliefs and norms can influence the development and expression of phobias. Certain cultures may have specific fears that are more prevalent due to cultural narratives or societal attitudes.

Psychological Factors

PSYCHOLOGICAL FACTORS, including individual temperament and personality traits, can also contribute to the development of phobias. Some key psychological factors include:

1. Temperament: Individuals with certain temperamental traits, such as high levels of behavioral inhibition (a tendency to be shy, cautious, and avoidant), are more likely to develop phobias. These traits can make individuals more sensitive to fear and less likely to engage in new or unfamiliar situations.

2. Cognitive Biases: Cognitive biases, such as the tendency to overestimate danger or perceive situations as more threatening than they are, can contribute to the development and maintenance of phobias. These biases can lead to heightened anxiety and avoidance behaviors.

3. Emotional Regulation: Difficulty regulating emotions and coping with stress can increase the likelihood of developing phobias. Individuals who struggle with emotional regulation may be more prone to experiencing intense fear and anxiety in response to stressors.

How Phobias Develop and Manifest

PHOBIAS TYPICALLY DEVELOP through a combination of genetic, environmental, and psychological factors, and they can manifest in various ways. Understanding the development and manifestation of phobias can help individuals recognize their symptoms and seek appropriate treatment.

Development of Phobias

PHOBIAS OFTEN DEVELOP during childhood or adolescence, but they can also emerge in adulthood. The development of phobias can be influenced by several key processes:

1. Classical Conditioning: Classical conditioning is a process in which a neutral stimulus becomes associated with a fearful response. For example, if a child is bitten by a dog, the experience of pain and fear becomes associated with the sight of dogs, leading to a lasting fear of dogs. This learned association can persist even after the original threat is no longer present.

2. Operant Conditioning: Operant conditioning involves the reinforcement of behaviors through rewards or punishments. In the context of phobias, avoidance behaviors are negatively reinforced because they reduce anxiety. For example, if someone with a fear of flying avoids airplanes, the immediate reduction in anxiety reinforces the avoidance behavior, making it more likely to continue.

3. Observational Learning: Observational learning occurs when individuals learn to fear certain objects or situations by observing others' fearful reactions. For example, a child who sees a parent react fearfully to spiders may develop a fear of spiders themselves. This process can be particularly influential during childhood when individuals are more susceptible to learning from their environment.

4. Information Transmission: Phobias can also develop through the transmission of information, such as hearing about dangers from others or consuming media that portrays certain objects or situations as threatening. For

example, repeated exposure to news reports about plane crashes can contribute to the development of a fear of flying.

Manifestation of Phobias

PHOBIAS CAN MANIFEST in various ways, and the symptoms can range from mild to severe. Common manifestations of phobias include:

1. Physical Symptoms: Physical symptoms of phobias are similar to those experienced during anxiety and panic attacks. These can include increased heart rate, sweating, trembling, shortness of breath, dizziness, and gastrointestinal distress. These symptoms can occur when the individual is exposed to the feared object or situation, or even when thinking about it.

2. Behavioral Symptoms: Behavioral symptoms of phobias primarily involve avoidance behaviors. Individuals may go to great lengths to avoid the feared object or situation, which can significantly interfere with daily life. For example, someone with a fear of flying may refuse to travel by plane, even if it limits their personal or professional opportunities.

3. Cognitive Symptoms: Cognitive symptoms of phobias involve persistent and irrational thoughts about the feared object or situation. These thoughts can include overestimations of danger, catastrophizing, and the belief that one cannot cope with the fear. For example, someone with social phobia may believe that they will embarrass themselves in social situations and that others will judge them harshly.

4. Emotional Symptoms: Emotional symptoms of phobias include intense fear, anxiety, and panic when exposed to the feared object or situation. These emotions can be overwhelming and difficult to manage, leading to significant distress and impairment in daily functioning.

Case Studies and Examples

UNDERSTANDING PHOBIAS through real-life examples can provide valuable insight into how these disorders develop and manifest. The following case studies illustrate the experiences of individuals with specific phobias, social phobia, and agoraphobia.

Case Study 1: Specific Phobia

BACKGROUND: SARAH IS a 30-year-old woman who has had a severe fear of spiders (arachnophobia) since childhood. Her fear began after a traumatic incident when she was five years old and a spider crawled onto her face while she was sleeping.

Symptoms: Sarah experiences intense fear and panic whenever she sees a spider, even if it is at a distance or in a picture. Her physical symptoms include increased heart rate, sweating, trembling, and shortness of breath. She also has persistent and irrational thoughts about spiders being dangerous and believes that they could harm her.

Behavioral Impact: Sarah goes to great lengths to avoid spiders. She avoids areas where spiders are likely to be present, such as basements, attics, and wooded areas. She also checks her home regularly for spiders and uses insecticide sprays to keep them away. Her avoidance behaviors have become so severe that she has stopped visiting friends and family who live in rural areas where spiders are more common.

Treatment: Sarah sought treatment for her phobia and began exposure therapy, a type of cognitive-behavioral therapy (CBT) that involves gradual and controlled exposure to the feared object. With the help of her therapist, Sarah created an exposure hierarchy, starting with looking at pictures of spiders and gradually progressing to being in the same room as a live spider. Over time, her fear and avoidance behaviors diminished, and she was able to resume her normal activities.

Case Study 2: Social Phobia

BACKGROUND: MARK IS a 25-year-old man who has struggled with social anxiety disorder since high school. He fears social interactions and worries about being judged or embarrassed by others.

Symptoms: Mark experiences intense fear and anxiety in social situations, such as parties, meetings, and public speaking. His physical symptoms include sweating, trembling, blushing, and an increased heart rate. He also has persistent negative thoughts, such as believing that others are judging him or that he will say something embarrassing.

Behavioral Impact: Mark's social anxiety has led to significant avoidance behaviors. He avoids social gatherings, declines invitations to events, and has difficulty participating in group activities at work. His fear of public speaking has also affected his career, as he avoids presenting his ideas in meetings or speaking in front of colleagues.

Treatment: Mark sought help from a therapist who specialized in cognitive-behavioral therapy (CBT). Through CBT, Mark learned to identify and challenge his negative thought patterns and gradually faced his fears through exposure exercises. He practiced speaking in front of small groups, gradually increasing the audience size. Over time, Mark's confidence in social situations improved, and he was able to engage more comfortably in social interactions and professional settings.

Case Study 3: Agoraphobia

BACKGROUND: EMILY IS a 40-year-old woman who developed agoraphobia after experiencing several panic attacks in public places. Her fear of having a panic attack in situations where escape might be difficult led to severe avoidance behaviors.

Symptoms: Emily experiences intense fear and anxiety when she is in situations where she feels trapped or unable to escape, such as crowded places, public transportation, and open spaces. Her physical symptoms during these episodes include heart palpitations, shortness of breath, dizziness, and a sense of impending doom.

Behavioral Impact: Emily's agoraphobia has led to significant impairment in her daily life. She avoids leaving her home and relies on family members to run errands and take her to appointments. Her fear of public transportation has also limited her ability to travel and attend social events.

Treatment: Emily sought treatment from a therapist who used a combination of cognitive-behavioral therapy (CBT) and exposure therapy. Through CBT, Emily learned to identify and challenge her catastrophic thinking patterns. She also participated in gradual exposure exercises, starting with short trips outside her home and gradually increasing the duration and complexity of the situations. With the support of her therapist and family, Emily made significant progress and was able to regain her independence and participate in activities she had previously avoided.

Treatment and Coping Strategies

PHOBIAS CAN BE EFFECTIVELY treated through a variety of therapeutic approaches. The most common and evidence-based treatments include cognitive-behavioral therapy (CBT), exposure therapy, and medication. Additionally, self-help strategies and coping mechanisms can help individuals manage their symptoms and improve their quality of life.

Cognitive-Behavioral Therapy (CBT)

CBT IS A WIDELY USED and effective treatment for phobias. It focuses on identifying and challenging irrational thought patterns and beliefs that contribute to fear and avoidance behaviors. Key components of CBT for phobias include:

1. Cognitive Restructuring: This involves identifying and challenging negative thought patterns and cognitive distortions, such as catastrophizing or overestimating danger. By reframing these thoughts, individuals can reduce their fear and anxiety.

2. Behavioral Experiments: Behavioral experiments involve testing the validity of negative beliefs through real-life experiences. For example, someone with a fear of public speaking might give a short presentation and observe that their feared outcomes (e.g., being judged harshly) do not occur.

3. Exposure Exercises: Exposure exercises involve gradually and systematically facing the feared object or situation. This can be done through imaginal exposure (visualizing the feared situation) or in vivo exposure (real-life exposure). The goal is to reduce fear and avoidance behaviors over time.

Exposure Therapy

EXPOSURE THERAPY IS a specific type of CBT that focuses on gradual and controlled exposure to the feared object or situation. The process involves creating an exposure hierarchy, which is a list of feared situations ranked by their intensity. The individual then works through the hierarchy, starting with the least fear-inducing situation and gradually progressing to the most fear-inducing.

Key steps in exposure therapy include:

1. Creating an Exposure Hierarchy: The individual and therapist collaborate to identify feared situations and rank them in order of intensity. This hierarchy serves as a roadmap for exposure exercises.

2. Gradual Exposure: The individual begins with the least fear-inducing situation and gradually works their way up the hierarchy. Exposure can be done in real life (in vivo exposure) or through visualization (imaginal exposure).

3. Sustained Exposure: Each exposure exercise should be sustained until the individual's anxiety decreases. This helps to reinforce that the feared situation is not as threatening as initially believed.

4. Repeated Exposure: Repeated exposure to the feared situation helps to desensitize the individual to their fear and reduce avoidance behaviors.

Medication

Medication can be an effective adjunct to therapy for individuals with severe or persistent phobias. Commonly prescribed medications for phobias include:

1. Selective Serotonin Reuptake Inhibitors (SSRIs): SSRIs, such as fluoxetine (Prozac) and sertraline (Zoloft), are commonly used to treat anxiety disorders.

They work by increasing serotonin levels in the brain, which can help to reduce anxiety.

2. Benzodiazepines: Benzodiazepines, such as diazepam (Valium) and alprazolam (Xanax), are fast-acting medications that can provide short-term relief from anxiety symptoms. However, they are typically prescribed for short-term use due to the risk of dependence and withdrawal.

3. Beta-Blockers: Beta-blockers, such as propranolol (Inderal), can help to reduce physical symptoms of anxiety, such as rapid heart rate and trembling. They are often used on an as-needed basis for situational anxiety, such as public speaking.

Self-Help Strategies and Coping Mechanisms

IN ADDITION TO PROFESSIONAL treatment, self-help strategies and coping mechanisms can play a crucial role in managing phobias. Some effective self-help strategies include:

1. Relaxation Techniques: Practicing relaxation techniques, such as deep breathing, progressive muscle relaxation, and mindfulness meditation, can help to reduce anxiety and promote a sense of calm.

2. Exercise: Regular physical activity can help to reduce anxiety by releasing endorphins and promoting overall well-being. Activities such as yoga, walking, and swimming can be particularly beneficial.

3. Healthy Lifestyle: Maintaining a healthy lifestyle, including a balanced diet, adequate sleep, and limited caffeine and alcohol intake, can help to reduce anxiety and improve overall mental health.

4. Support Networks: Building a support network of family, friends, and support groups can provide emotional support and encouragement. Sharing experiences with others who understand can help to reduce feelings of isolation.

5. Positive Self-Talk: Practicing positive self-talk and affirmations can help to counteract negative thought patterns and boost self-confidence.

6. Gradual Exposure: Gradual exposure to feared situations, even without formal therapy, can help to reduce avoidance behaviors and desensitize individuals to their fears.

Conclusion

Phobias are a common and treatable form of anxiety disorder that can significantly impact an individual's daily life. By understanding the different types of phobias, their causes and risk factors, and how they develop and manifest, individuals can gain insight into their experiences and seek appropriate treatment.

Effective treatments for phobias include cognitive-behavioral therapy (CBT), exposure therapy, and medication. Additionally, self-help strategies and coping mechanisms can help individuals manage their symptoms and improve their quality of life.

Recognizing and addressing phobias is an important step towards overcoming fear and living a fulfilling life. With the right knowledge, resources, and support, individuals can take control of their phobias and work towards a future free from excessive fear and avoidance.

Chapter 3: The Anxiety-Phobia Connection

How Anxiety and Phobias Interact

Anxiety and phobias are deeply interconnected, often creating a self-perpetuating cycle that can be challenging to break. Understanding how these conditions interact is crucial for developing effective strategies to manage and overcome them. This chapter explores the relationship between anxiety and phobias, the vicious cycle of fear and avoidance, case studies illustrating the connection, and methods for breaking the cycle.

The Vicious Cycle of Fear and Avoidance

THE INTERACTION BETWEEN anxiety and phobias often forms a vicious cycle of fear and avoidance. This cycle can be understood through the following components:

1. Triggering Event or Situation: The cycle often begins with exposure to a triggering event or situation that elicits a fear response. For individuals with phobias, this could be an encounter with the feared object or situation, such as seeing a spider for someone with arachnophobia.

2. Immediate Anxiety Response: The triggering event leads to an immediate anxiety response, characterized by physical symptoms such as increased heart rate, sweating, and trembling, as well as cognitive symptoms like catastrophic thinking and a sense of impending doom.

3. Avoidance Behavior: To alleviate the anxiety, individuals engage in avoidance behaviors, such as leaving the situation, avoiding places where the trigger might be present, or taking specific actions to prevent exposure (e.g., checking for spiders before entering a room).

4. Short-Term Relief: Avoidance behavior provides short-term relief from anxiety, reinforcing the behavior and making it more likely to occur in the

future. This negative reinforcement strengthens the association between the trigger and the need to avoid it.

5. Long-Term Consequences: Over time, avoidance behaviors can lead to increased sensitivity to the feared object or situation, as well as broader impacts on daily functioning. The individual may start to avoid a wider range of situations, leading to significant impairment in personal, social, and professional life.

6. Increased Anxiety and Fear: The ongoing cycle of avoidance and short-term relief ultimately increases overall anxiety and fear. The individual becomes more vigilant and anticipatory of potential triggers, leading to heightened anxiety and more frequent avoidance behaviors.

Case Studies Illustrating the Connection

EXAMINING REAL-LIFE case studies can provide a deeper understanding of how anxiety and phobias interact and perpetuate the cycle of fear and avoidance. The following case studies illustrate the experiences of individuals with specific phobias, social phobia, and agoraphobia, highlighting the interplay between anxiety and phobias.

Case Study 1: Specific Phobia (Arachnophobia)

BACKGROUND: EMMA IS a 35-year-old woman with a severe fear of spiders (arachnophobia). Her phobia began in childhood after a traumatic incident in which a large spider crawled onto her while she was sleeping.

Triggering Event: Emma encounters a spider in her bathroom.

Immediate Anxiety Response: Upon seeing the spider, Emma experiences intense fear and anxiety. Her physical symptoms include a rapid heart rate, sweating, and trembling. She also has catastrophic thoughts, such as imagining the spider crawling on her and biting her.

Avoidance Behavior: To escape the anxiety, Emma quickly leaves the bathroom and avoids using it until she is certain the spider is gone. She asks her partner to remove the spider, reinforcing her avoidance behavior.

Short-Term Relief: Once the spider is removed and Emma feels it is safe to return to the bathroom, her anxiety decreases, providing immediate relief.

Long-Term Consequences: Over time, Emma becomes increasingly vigilant and fearful of encountering spiders. She begins to avoid other areas where spiders might be present, such as basements, garages, and outdoor spaces. Her avoidance behavior generalizes, leading to a significant impact on her daily life and limiting her activities.

Increased Anxiety and Fear: Emma's ongoing avoidance and hypervigilance lead to heightened overall anxiety and a more intense fear response whenever she encounters or thinks about spiders. Her world becomes increasingly restricted as she avoids more situations.

Case Study 2: Social Phobia (Social Anxiety Disorder)

BACKGROUND: JOHN IS a 28-year-old man with social anxiety disorder. His fear of social interactions began in adolescence, particularly during high school, when he was often criticized and judged by his peers.

Triggering Event: John is invited to a friend's party.

Immediate Anxiety Response: The thought of attending the party triggers intense anxiety for John. He worries about being judged, saying something embarrassing, or being the center of attention. His physical symptoms include sweating, a racing heart, and a feeling of nausea.

Avoidance Behavior: To avoid the anxiety, John declines the invitation and stays home. He tells his friend that he is not feeling well, providing an excuse to avoid the social interaction.

Short-Term Relief: By avoiding the party, John experiences immediate relief from his anxiety, reinforcing his decision to avoid social situations in the future.

Long-Term Consequences: Over time, John's avoidance behavior leads to increased isolation and loneliness. He misses out on social opportunities, friendships, and professional networking events. His fear of social interactions generalizes, making it difficult for him to engage in even small group settings.

Increased Anxiety and Fear: John's ongoing avoidance leads to heightened overall anxiety and a more intense fear response to social situations. He becomes more self-conscious and anticipatory of negative social outcomes, further reinforcing his avoidance behavior.

Case Study 3: Agoraphobia

BACKGROUND: LISA IS a 45-year-old woman with agoraphobia, which developed after experiencing several panic attacks in public places. Her fear of having a panic attack in situations where escape might be difficult has led to significant avoidance behaviors.

Triggering Event: Lisa needs to go grocery shopping.

Immediate Anxiety Response: The thought of going to the grocery store triggers intense anxiety for Lisa. She worries about having a panic attack in the store and being unable to escape. Her physical symptoms include a racing heart, shortness of breath, and dizziness.

Avoidance Behavior: To avoid the anxiety, Lisa decides to order groceries online instead of going to the store. She avoids leaving her home and relies on delivery services for her shopping needs.

Short-Term Relief: By avoiding the grocery store, Lisa experiences immediate relief from her anxiety, reinforcing her decision to avoid public places in the future.

Long-Term Consequences: Over time, Lisa's avoidance behavior leads to increased dependence on others and a significant reduction in her daily activities. She avoids other public places, such as malls, restaurants, and public transportation, further restricting her life.

Increased Anxiety and Fear: Lisa's ongoing avoidance leads to heightened overall anxiety and a more intense fear response to public places. She becomes increasingly isolated and dependent on others, making it difficult for her to regain her independence.

Breaking the Cycle

BREAKING THE CYCLE of fear and avoidance requires a comprehensive approach that addresses both the cognitive and behavioral aspects of anxiety and phobias. The following strategies and techniques can help individuals break free from the vicious cycle and regain control over their lives.

Cognitive-Behavioral Therapy (CBT)

COGNITIVE-BEHAVIORAL therapy (CBT) is a widely used and effective treatment for anxiety and phobias. It focuses on identifying and challenging irrational thought patterns and beliefs that contribute to fear and avoidance behaviors. Key components of CBT for breaking the cycle include:

1. Cognitive Restructuring: This involves identifying and challenging negative thought patterns and cognitive distortions, such as catastrophizing or overestimating danger. By reframing these thoughts, individuals can reduce their fear and anxiety. For example, someone with social phobia might challenge the belief that others are judging them harshly and reframe it as a more realistic and balanced thought.

2. Behavioral Experiments: Behavioral experiments involve testing the validity of negative beliefs through real-life experiences. For example, someone with a fear of public speaking might give a short presentation and observe that their feared outcomes (e.g., being judged harshly) do not occur. This helps to challenge and change irrational beliefs.

3. Exposure Exercises: Exposure exercises involve gradually and systematically facing the feared object or situation. This can be done through imaginal exposure (visualizing the feared situation) or in vivo exposure (real-life exposure). The goal is to reduce fear and avoidance behaviors over time. For

example, someone with agoraphobia might start with short trips outside their home and gradually increase the duration and complexity of the situations.

Exposure Therapy

EXPOSURE THERAPY IS a specific type of CBT that focuses on gradual and controlled exposure to the feared object or situation. The process involves creating an exposure hierarchy, which is a list of feared situations ranked by their intensity. The individual then works through the hierarchy, starting with the least fear-inducing situation and gradually progressing to the most fear-inducing. Key steps in exposure therapy include:

1. Creating an Exposure Hierarchy: The individual and therapist collaborate to identify feared situations and rank them in order of intensity. This hierarchy serves as a roadmap for exposure exercises. For example, someone with a fear of flying might start with looking at pictures of airplanes and gradually progress to taking a short flight.

2. Gradual Exposure: The individual begins with the least fear-inducing situation and gradually works their way up the hierarchy. Exposure can be done in real life (in vivo exposure) or through visualization (imaginal exposure). For example, someone with a fear of spiders might start with looking at pictures of spiders and gradually progress to being in the same room as a live spider.

3. Sustained Exposure: Each exposure exercise should be sustained until the individual's anxiety decreases. This helps to reinforce that the feared situation is not as threatening as initially believed. For example, someone with social phobia might practice speaking in front of a small group until their anxiety decreases.

4. Repeated Exposure: Repeated exposure to the feared situation helps to desensitize the individual to their fear and reduce avoidance behaviors. For example, someone with agoraphobia might practice going to the grocery store regularly until their anxiety decreases.

Medication

Medication can be an effective adjunct to therapy for individuals with severe or persistent anxiety and phobias. Commonly prescribed medications for anxiety and phobias include:

1. Selective Serotonin Reuptake Inhibitors (SSRIs): SSRIs, such as fluoxetine (Prozac) and sertraline (Zoloft), are commonly used to treat anxiety disorders. They work by increasing serotonin levels in the brain, which can help to reduce anxiety.

2. Benzodiazepines: Benzodiazepines, such as diazepam (Valium) and alprazolam (Xanax), are fast-acting medications that can provide short-term relief from anxiety symptoms. However, they are typically prescribed for short-term use due to the risk of dependence and withdrawal.

3. Beta-Blockers: Beta-blockers, such as propranolol (Inderal), can help to reduce physical symptoms of anxiety, such as rapid heart rate and trembling. They are often used on an as-needed basis for situational anxiety, such as public speaking.

Mindfulness and Relaxation Techniques

PRACTICING MINDFULNESS and relaxation techniques can help individuals manage anxiety and reduce the intensity of their fear response. These techniques include:

1. Mindfulness Meditation: Mindfulness meditation involves paying attention to the present moment without judgment. This practice can help individuals become more aware of their thoughts and feelings and develop a more accepting and non-reactive attitude towards them. Regular mindfulness meditation can reduce overall anxiety and improve emotional regulation.

2. Deep Breathing: Deep breathing exercises, such as diaphragmatic breathing, can help to activate the body's relaxation response and reduce physical symptoms of anxiety. Practicing deep breathing regularly can help individuals manage their anxiety more effectively.

3. Progressive Muscle Relaxation: Progressive muscle relaxation involves tensing and relaxing different muscle groups in the body. This technique can help to reduce physical tension and promote a sense of calm. Practicing progressive muscle relaxation regularly can help individuals manage their anxiety more effectively.

Healthy Lifestyle and Self-Care

MAINTAINING A HEALTHY lifestyle and practicing self-care can also play a crucial role in managing anxiety and breaking the cycle of fear and avoidance. Key components of a healthy lifestyle include:

1. Regular Exercise: Regular physical activity can help to reduce anxiety by releasing endorphins and promoting overall well-being. Activities such as yoga, walking, and swimming can be particularly beneficial.

2. Balanced Diet: Eating a balanced diet that includes a variety of nutrients can help to support overall mental health. Avoiding excessive caffeine and sugar can also help to reduce anxiety.

3. Adequate Sleep: Getting enough sleep is essential for managing anxiety. Establishing a regular sleep routine and creating a relaxing bedtime environment can help to improve sleep quality.

4. Stress Management: Practicing stress management techniques, such as time management, prioritization, and setting boundaries, can help to reduce overall stress and anxiety.

5. Social Support: Building and maintaining a support network of family, friends, and support groups can provide emotional support and encouragement. Sharing experiences with others who understand can help to reduce feelings of isolation.

Conclusion

Anxiety and phobias are deeply interconnected, often creating a vicious cycle of fear and avoidance that can be challenging to break. Understanding how these conditions interact and perpetuate each other is crucial for developing effective strategies to manage and overcome them.

Through cognitive-behavioral therapy (CBT), exposure therapy, medication, mindfulness and relaxation techniques, and maintaining a healthy lifestyle, individuals can break the cycle of fear and avoidance and regain control over their lives. By addressing both the cognitive and behavioral aspects of anxiety and phobias, individuals can develop the skills and resilience needed to navigate their fears and lead a fulfilling life.

Remember, breaking the cycle of fear and avoidance is a gradual process that requires patience, persistence, and support. With the right knowledge, resources, and strategies, individuals can overcome their anxiety and phobias and work towards a future free from excessive fear and avoidance.

Chapter 4: Self-Assessment and Diagnosis

Identifying Your Triggers

Self-assessment and understanding your own anxiety and phobia triggers are crucial steps toward managing these conditions effectively. Recognizing what provokes your anxiety can help you develop coping strategies and determine when professional help is necessary. This chapter will cover various self-assessment tools and questionnaires, guide you on when to seek professional help, and explain how to understand your diagnosis.

Self-Assessment Tools and Questionnaires

SELF-ASSESSMENT TOOLS and questionnaires are designed to help you identify the presence and severity of anxiety and phobias. These tools can provide insight into your symptoms and help you understand whether your anxiety or phobia might require professional intervention. Here are some widely used self-assessment tools:

Generalized Anxiety Disorder 7 (GAD-7)

THE GAD-7 IS A BRIEF, seven-item questionnaire used to screen for generalized anxiety disorder and measure its severity. Each question asks how often you have been bothered by certain problems over the past two weeks, with responses ranging from "not at all" to "nearly every day."

Questions include:

1. FEELING NERVOUS, anxious, or on edge.

2. Not being able to stop or control worrying.

3. Worrying too much about different things.

4. Trouble relaxing.

5. Being so restless that it is hard to sit still.

6. Becoming easily annoyed or irritable.

7. Feeling afraid as if something awful might happen.

Scoring:

- 0-4: Minimal anxiety

- 5-9: Mild anxiety

- 10-14: Moderate anxiety

- 15-21: Severe anxiety

Social Phobia Inventory (SPIN)

THE SPIN IS A 17-ITEM questionnaire designed to identify social anxiety disorder (social phobia) and assess its severity. Each item is rated on a scale from 0 (not at all) to 4 (extremely), based on how much the problem has bothered you in the past week.

Questions include:

1. FEAR OF PEOPLE IN authority.

2. Fear of being embarrassed.

3. Avoiding activities where you are the center of attention.

4. Worrying about trembling or shaking.

5. Avoiding social situations where you might be judged.

Scoring:

- 0-20: Mild social anxiety

- 21-40: Moderate social anxiety

- 41-60: Severe social anxiety

Panic Disorder Severity Scale (PDSS)

THE PDSS IS USED TO assess the severity of panic disorder. It consists of seven items that evaluate the frequency and intensity of panic attacks, as well as the impact on daily functioning.

Questions include:

1. FREQUENCY OF PANIC attacks.

2. Distress during panic attacks.

3. Avoidance of situations due to fear of panic attacks.

4. Fear of losing control or going crazy during a panic attack.

Scoring:

Each item is rated on a scale from 0 (none) to 4 (extreme), and the total score determines the severity of panic disorder.

Specific Phobia Inventory (SPI)

THE SPI HELPS IDENTIFY and measure the severity of specific phobias. It consists of questions tailored to different types of phobias, such as fear of animals, natural environments, blood-injection-injury, or situational fears.

Questions include:

1. FREQUENCY OF ENCOUNTERING the feared object or situation.

2. Level of fear experienced when thinking about or encountering the phobic stimulus.

3. Avoidance behaviors related to the phobia.

Scoring:

Each item is rated on a scale from 0 (none) to 4 (extreme), and the total score indicates the severity of the specific phobia.

When to Seek Professional Help

WHILE SELF-ASSESSMENT tools can provide valuable insights, they are not a substitute for professional evaluation. It is essential to know when to seek professional help for anxiety and phobias. Here are some indicators that professional intervention might be necessary:

Severity and Persistence of Symptoms

IF YOUR ANXIETY OR phobia symptoms are severe, persistent, and significantly interfere with your daily life, it is crucial to seek professional help. This includes symptoms that:

- Cause significant distress or impairment in social, occupational, or other important areas of functioning.

- Persist for six months or longer.

- Do not improve with self-help strategies or coping mechanisms.

Impact on Daily Functioning

IF YOUR ANXIETY OR phobia prevents you from engaging in normal daily activities, it is a sign that professional help is needed. Examples include:

- Avoiding work or school due to anxiety or phobias.

- Difficulty maintaining personal relationships or participating in social activities.

- Inability to perform routine tasks, such as grocery shopping or using public transportation.

Physical Symptoms

IF YOU EXPERIENCE SEVERE physical symptoms related to anxiety or phobias, it is important to consult a healthcare professional. These symptoms can include:

- Panic attacks with intense physical symptoms such as chest pain, dizziness, or shortness of breath.

- Significant weight loss or gain due to anxiety-related eating patterns.

- Chronic headaches, gastrointestinal issues, or other physical complaints.

Co-occurring Mental Health Conditions

IF YOU HAVE CO-OCCURRING mental health conditions, such as depression, substance abuse, or another anxiety disorder, professional help is essential for comprehensive treatment. These conditions can complicate the diagnosis and management of anxiety and phobias, requiring a coordinated approach.

Suicidal Thoughts or Behaviors

IF YOU EXPERIENCE SUICIDAL thoughts or behaviors, seek immediate professional help. Suicidal ideation is a serious symptom that requires urgent intervention. Contact a mental health professional, crisis hotline, or emergency services if you are in immediate danger.

Understanding Your Diagnosis

ONCE YOU SEEK PROFESSIONAL help, a mental health professional will conduct a thorough evaluation to diagnose your anxiety or phobia.

Understanding your diagnosis is a crucial step toward effective treatment and management. Here is an overview of the diagnostic process and what to expect:

Initial Assessment

THE INITIAL ASSESSMENT typically involves a comprehensive interview to gather information about your symptoms, medical history, and any contributing factors. During this assessment, the mental health professional may ask about:

- The nature, frequency, and duration of your symptoms.

- Situations or triggers that provoke anxiety or phobic reactions.

- Your family history of mental health conditions.

- Any past or current treatments you have received.

- Your overall physical health and any medical conditions.

Diagnostic Criteria

MENTAL HEALTH PROFESSIONALS use standardized criteria to diagnose anxiety disorders and phobias. The Diagnostic and Statistical Manual of Mental Disorders, Fifth Edition (DSM-5), published by the American Psychiatric Association, provides the criteria for diagnosing these conditions. Here are the criteria for some common anxiety disorders and phobias:

Generalized Anxiety Disorder (GAD):

- Excessive anxiety and worry occurring more days than not for at least six months, about a number of events or activities.

- Difficulty controlling the worry.

- The anxiety and worry are associated with three or more of the following symptoms:

- Restlessness or feeling on edge.

- Being easily fatigued.

- Difficulty concentrating or mind going blank.

- Irritability.

- Muscle tension.

- Sleep disturbances.

Social Anxiety Disorder (Social Phobia):

- Marked fear or anxiety about one or more social situations in which the individual is exposed to possible scrutiny by others.

- The individual fears that they will act in a way or show anxiety symptoms that will be negatively evaluated.

- The social situations almost always provoke fear or anxiety.

- The social situations are avoided or endured with intense fear or anxiety.

- The fear or anxiety is out of proportion to the actual threat posed by the social situation.

- The fear, anxiety, or avoidance is persistent, typically lasting for six months or more.

- The fear, anxiety, or avoidance causes clinically significant distress or impairment in social, occupational, or other important areas of functioning.

Panic Disorder:

- Recurrent unexpected panic attacks, which are abrupt surges of intense fear or discomfort that reach a peak within minutes.

- At least one of the attacks is followed by one month (or more) of one or both of the following:

- Persistent concern or worry about additional panic attacks or their consequences.

- A significant maladaptive change in behavior related to the attacks (e.g., behaviors designed to avoid having panic attacks).

Specific Phobias:

- Marked fear or anxiety about a specific object or situation.

- The phobic object or situation almost always provokes immediate fear or anxiety.

- The phobic object or situation is actively avoided or endured with intense fear or anxiety.

- The fear or anxiety is out of proportion to the actual danger posed by the specific object or situation.

- The fear, anxiety, or avoidance is persistent, typically lasting for six months or more.

- The fear, anxiety, or avoidance causes clinically significant distress or impairment in social, occupational, or other important areas of functioning.

Agoraphobia:

- Marked fear or anxiety about two (or more) of the following five situations:

- Using public transportation.

- Being in open spaces.

- Being in enclosed spaces.

- Standing in line or being in a crowd.

- Being outside of the home alone.

- The individual fears or avoids these situations due to thoughts that escape might be difficult or help might not be available in the event of developing panic-like symptoms or other incapacitating or embarrassing symptoms.

- The agoraphobic situations almost always provoke fear or anxiety.

- The agoraphobic situations are actively avoided, require the presence of a companion, or are endured with intense fear or anxiety.

- The fear or anxiety is out of proportion to the actual danger posed by the agoraphobic situations.

- The fear, anxiety, or avoidance is persistent, typically lasting for six months or more.

- The fear, anxiety, or avoidance causes clinically significant distress or impairment in social, occupational, or other important areas of functioning.

Differential Diagnosis

DURING THE DIAGNOSTIC process, the mental health professional will also consider differential diagnoses. This involves ruling out other mental health conditions or medical issues that might present with similar symptoms. Some conditions that can mimic anxiety disorders and phobias include:

- Depression: Symptoms of depression, such as fatigue, irritability, and difficulty concentrating, can overlap with anxiety disorders.

- Obsessive-Compulsive Disorder (OCD): OCD involves intrusive thoughts (obsessions) and repetitive behaviors (compulsions) that can cause significant anxiety.

- Post-Traumatic Stress Disorder (PTSD): PTSD involves anxiety and fear responses related to a traumatic event.

- Medical Conditions: Certain medical conditions, such as thyroid disorders, cardiovascular issues, or gastrointestinal problems, can cause symptoms that resemble anxiety. A thorough evaluation helps ensure an accurate diagnosis and appropriate treatment plan.

Understanding Your Diagnosis

ONCE YOU RECEIVE A diagnosis, understanding its implications is essential for effective management. Here are some key aspects to consider:

1. Educational Resources: Educate yourself about your diagnosis by seeking reliable sources of information. This includes reading books, articles, and reputable websites that provide evidence-based information about anxiety disorders and phobias.

2. Treatment Options: Learn about the various treatment options available for your diagnosis. These may include psychotherapy (such as cognitive-behavioral therapy), medication, lifestyle changes, and self-help strategies. Understanding your treatment options empowers you to make informed decisions about your care.

3. Prognosis: Understanding the prognosis of your condition can help set realistic expectations for your recovery. While anxiety disorders and phobias are highly treatable, the duration and outcome of treatment can vary depending on individual factors, such as the severity of symptoms and the presence of co-occurring conditions.

4. Support Systems: Recognize the importance of building a support system to aid in your recovery. This can include family, friends, support groups, and mental health professionals. Having a strong support network can provide emotional support, encouragement, and practical assistance.

5. Self-Advocacy: Advocate for yourself by communicating openly with your mental health professional about your symptoms, concerns, and treatment preferences. Being an active participant in your care can enhance the effectiveness of your treatment and improve your overall well-being.

Practical Tips for Managing Anxiety and Phobias

IN ADDITION TO SEEKING professional help and understanding your diagnosis, there are practical steps you can take to manage anxiety and phobias effectively. Here are some self-help strategies and coping mechanisms:

Relaxation Techniques

PRACTICING RELAXATION techniques can help reduce anxiety and promote a sense of calm. Some effective relaxation techniques include:

1. Deep Breathing: Practice diaphragmatic breathing by inhaling deeply through your nose, allowing your abdomen to expand, and exhaling slowly through your mouth. Repeat this several times to calm your nervous system.

2. Progressive Muscle Relaxation: Tense and relax different muscle groups in your body, starting from your toes and working your way up to your head. This technique can help release physical tension and reduce anxiety.

3. Guided Imagery: Use guided imagery to visualize calming and peaceful scenes. Close your eyes and imagine yourself in a relaxing environment, such as a beach or a forest. Engage your senses by imagining the sights, sounds, and smells of the scene.

Mindfulness and Meditation

MINDFULNESS AND MEDITATION practices can help you stay present and reduce anxiety. Some techniques to try include:

1. Mindfulness Meditation: Sit quietly and focus on your breath, observing each inhale and exhale without judgment. When your mind wanders, gently bring your attention back to your breath.

2. Body Scan Meditation: Lie down or sit comfortably and bring your attention to different parts of your body, starting from your toes and working your way up to your head. Notice any sensations, tension, or relaxation in each area.

3. Mindful Walking: Take a walk and focus on the sensation of your feet touching the ground, the movement of your body, and the sights and sounds around you. Practice being fully present in the moment.

Physical Activity

REGULAR PHYSICAL ACTIVITY can help reduce anxiety by releasing endorphins and improving overall well-being. Some activities to consider include:

1. Aerobic Exercise: Engage in activities such as running, swimming, cycling, or dancing to increase your heart rate and release endorphins.

2. Yoga: Practice yoga to combine physical movement with mindfulness and relaxation. Yoga can help improve flexibility, strength, and mental clarity.

3. Walking: Take regular walks in nature or your neighborhood to clear your mind and reduce stress.

Healthy Lifestyle

MAINTAINING A HEALTHY lifestyle can support your mental health and reduce anxiety. Consider the following tips:

1. Balanced Diet: Eat a balanced diet that includes a variety of nutrients. Avoid excessive caffeine and sugar, which can contribute to anxiety.

2. Adequate Sleep: Establish a regular sleep routine and create a relaxing bedtime environment to improve sleep quality.

3. Stress Management: Practice stress management techniques, such as time management, prioritization, and setting boundaries.

Support Networks

BUILDING AND MAINTAINING a support network can provide emotional support and encouragement. Consider the following steps:

1. Family and Friends: Share your experiences and feelings with trusted family members and friends who can offer support and understanding.

2. Support Groups: Join support groups, either in-person or online, to connect with others who understand your experiences and can offer advice and encouragement.

3. Professional Support: Continue working with your mental health professional to develop and adjust your treatment plan as needed.

Conclusion

Self-assessment and understanding your triggers are essential steps toward managing anxiety and phobias effectively. By using self-assessment tools and questionnaires, you can gain insight into your symptoms and determine when professional help is necessary.

Seeking professional help is crucial when your symptoms are severe, persistent, or significantly impact your daily life. Understanding your diagnosis, including the diagnostic criteria and differential diagnoses, empowers you to make informed decisions about your treatment and management.

In addition to professional help, practical strategies such as relaxation techniques, mindfulness, physical activity, and maintaining a healthy lifestyle can help you manage anxiety and phobias. Building a strong support network of family, friends, and support groups can provide the emotional support and encouragement needed for your recovery.

Remember that managing anxiety and phobias is a journey that requires patience, persistence, and support. With the right knowledge, resources, and strategies, you can take control of your anxiety and phobias and work toward a future free from excessive fear and avoidance.

Chapter 5: Cognitive-Behavioral Techniques

Changing Thought Patterns

Cognitive-behavioral therapy (CBT) is a well-established and effective treatment for anxiety and phobias. It focuses on identifying and changing negative thought patterns and behaviors that contribute to anxiety. This chapter introduces CBT, offers practical exercises for challenging negative thoughts, and provides real-life applications and success stories to illustrate its effectiveness.

Introduction to Cognitive-Behavioral Therapy (CBT)

COGNITIVE-BEHAVIORAL therapy (CBT) is a structured, time-limited, and goal-oriented form of psychotherapy that aims to change patterns of thinking or behavior that are causing people's problems, and so change the way they feel. Developed in the 1960s by Aaron Beck, CBT is based on the cognitive model, which posits that our thoughts, feelings, and behaviors are interconnected. By changing negative thought patterns, we can alter our emotional responses and behaviors.

CBT is founded on several key principles:

1. Cognitive Distortions: These are biased ways of thinking about oneself and the world. Common cognitive distortions include catastrophizing, overgeneralizing, and black-and-white thinking. Identifying and challenging these distortions is a core component of CBT.

2. Behavioral Experiments: These are activities designed to test the validity of negative thoughts and beliefs. By engaging in these experiments, individuals can gather evidence to support or refute their cognitive distortions.

3. Exposure Therapy: This involves gradually facing feared situations in a controlled and systematic way. Exposure therapy helps individuals reduce their avoidance behaviors and learn that their fears are often unfounded.

4. Skills Training: CBT often includes teaching specific skills to manage anxiety, such as relaxation techniques, problem-solving strategies, and assertiveness training.

Practical Exercises for Challenging Negative Thoughts

CHALLENGING NEGATIVE thoughts is a central aspect of CBT. The following exercises can help you identify and change cognitive distortions, leading to a reduction in anxiety and an improvement in overall well-being.

Identifying Negative Thoughts

THE FIRST STEP IN CHALLENGING negative thoughts is to identify them. This involves paying attention to your inner dialogue and recognizing when negative thoughts arise. Keeping a thought diary can be helpful for this process. In your thought diary, record the following:

1. Situation: Describe the event or situation that triggered your negative thoughts.

2. Emotions: Note the emotions you felt in response to the situation (e.g., anxiety, sadness, anger).

3. Negative Thoughts: Write down the specific negative thoughts that went through your mind.

4. Cognitive Distortions: Identify any cognitive distortions present in your negative thoughts (e.g., catastrophizing, overgeneralizing).

By regularly recording your thoughts, you can begin to identify patterns and become more aware of your negative thinking habits.

Challenging Negative Thoughts

ONCE YOU HAVE IDENTIFIED your negative thoughts, the next step is to challenge them. This involves evaluating the evidence for and against your thoughts and considering alternative, more balanced perspectives. The following questions can help you challenge your negative thoughts:

1. What is the evidence for this thought?: Consider the facts that support your negative thought. Are there any concrete examples that back it up?

2. What is the evidence against this thought?: Look for evidence that contradicts your negative thought. Are there any facts or experiences that disprove it?

3. Is this thought based on facts or assumptions?: Determine whether your thought is grounded in reality or if it is based on assumptions or interpretations.

4. Are there alternative explanations?: Think about other possible explanations for the situation. Are there any more balanced or realistic ways to view it?

5. What is the worst that could happen?: Consider the worst-case scenario and evaluate its likelihood. How would you cope if it did happen?

6. What is the best that could happen?: Imagine the best-case scenario. How likely is it to occur?

7. What is the most likely outcome?: Assess the most realistic outcome of the situation. How does this compare to your negative thought?

By systematically evaluating your negative thoughts, you can begin to replace them with more balanced and realistic perspectives.

Behavioral Experiments

BEHAVIORAL EXPERIMENTS are designed to test the validity of your negative thoughts and beliefs through real-life experiences. These experiments involve identifying a negative thought or belief, predicting what will happen, and then testing it through an activity or exposure. Afterward, you compare the predicted outcome with the actual outcome.

Here is a step-by-step guide to conducting a behavioral experiment:

1. Identify a Negative Thought or Belief: Choose a specific negative thought or belief that you want to test. For example, "If I speak up in a meeting, everyone will think I'm incompetent."

2. Make a Prediction: Predict what you think will happen if you test this thought. For example, "I predict that if I speak up in the meeting, at least three people will give me negative feedback."

3. Design the Experiment: Plan an activity that will test your prediction. For example, "In the next meeting, I will share one of my ideas with the group."

4. Conduct the Experiment: Carry out the activity and observe what happens. Pay attention to people's reactions and any feedback you receive.

5. Record the Results: Write down the actual outcome of the experiment. For example, "I spoke up in the meeting, and I received positive feedback from two colleagues. No one gave me negative feedback."

6. Compare Predictions with Results: Compare your original prediction with the actual outcome. Reflect on what you learned from the experiment and how it challenges your negative thought.

By conducting behavioral experiments, you can gather evidence to challenge and change your negative thoughts and beliefs.

Real-Life Applications and Success Stories

TO ILLUSTRATE THE EFFECTIVENESS of CBT, here are real-life applications and success stories of individuals who have used cognitive-behavioral techniques to overcome anxiety and phobias.

Case Study 1: Overcoming Social Anxiety

BACKGROUND: SARAH IS a 30-year-old woman who has struggled with social anxiety since her teenage years. She fears social situations where she might be judged or embarrassed, such as parties, meetings, and public speaking. Her anxiety has led to significant avoidance behaviors, impacting her personal and professional life.

Identifying Negative Thoughts: Sarah kept a thought diary and identified several negative thoughts related to social situations, such as "Everyone will think I'm boring," "I'll embarrass myself," and "People will judge me negatively."

Challenging Negative Thoughts: With the help of her therapist, Sarah used the following questions to challenge her negative thoughts:

- What is the evidence for this thought? "I sometimes struggle to keep conversations going, but I have had positive social interactions in the past."

- What is the evidence against this thought? "I have friends who enjoy spending time with me and colleagues who value my contributions."

- Is this thought based on facts or assumptions? "It's an assumption that everyone will think I'm boring. I don't have concrete evidence for this."

- Are there alternative explanations? "People might be focused on their own thoughts and not judging me as harshly as I think."

- What is the worst that could happen? "If I embarrass myself, it might be uncomfortable, but I can cope with it and learn from the experience."

- What is the best that could happen? "I might have a positive interaction and enjoy myself."

- What is the most likely outcome? "The most likely outcome is that the interaction will be neutral or positive, and people will not judge me as harshly as I fear."

Behavioral Experiments: Sarah designed and conducted several behavioral experiments to test her negative thoughts. For example:

- In a meeting, she shared one of her ideas with the group. She predicted that at least three people would give her negative feedback, but the actual outcome was positive feedback from two colleagues and no negative feedback.

- She attended a friend's party and challenged herself to initiate conversations with at least three people. She predicted that she would embarrass herself and be judged, but the actual outcome was that she had enjoyable conversations and received positive feedback.

Results: Through identifying and challenging her negative thoughts and conducting behavioral experiments, Sarah's social anxiety significantly decreased. She became more confident in social situations, engaged in more social activities, and advanced in her career by participating more actively in meetings and presentations.

Case Study 2: Overcoming a Specific Phobia (Fear of Flying)

BACKGROUND: JOHN IS a 45-year-old man with a severe fear of flying (aviophobia). His phobia began after experiencing turbulence on a flight several years ago. His fear has led to avoidance behaviors, such as refusing to travel by plane, which has impacted his ability to visit family and attend work-related events.

Identifying Negative Thoughts: John kept a thought diary and identified several negative thoughts related to flying, such as "The plane will crash," "I won't be able to handle the anxiety," and "I'll have a panic attack and embarrass myself."

Challenging Negative Thoughts: With the help of his therapist, John used the following questions to challenge his negative thoughts:

- What is the evidence for this thought? "Turbulence is uncomfortable, but planes are designed to handle it, and crashes are extremely rare."

- What is the evidence against this thought? "Flying is statistically one of the safest modes of transportation. I've flown many times before without any issues."

- Is this thought based on facts or assumptions? "It's an assumption that the plane will crash. I don't have concrete evidence for this."

- Are there alternative explanations? "Turbulence is a normal part of flying and doesn't mean the plane is in danger."

- What is the worst that could happen? "If I feel anxious or have a panic attack, it will be uncomfortable, but I can use coping strategies to manage it."

- What is the best that could happen? "I might have a smooth flight and feel proud of myself for facing my fear."

- What is the most likely outcome? "The most likely outcome is that the flight will be uneventful, and I will manage my anxiety effectively."

Behavioral Experiments: John designed and conducted several behavioral experiments to test his negative thoughts. For example:

- He watched videos about how airplanes work and how turbulence is managed to gather evidence against his fear of crashing.

- He practiced relaxation techniques, such as deep breathing and progressive muscle relaxation, to use during the flight.

- He took a short flight with a friend for support, predicting that he would experience severe anxiety and embarrassment. The actual outcome was manageable anxiety, and he felt proud of himself for facing his fear.

Results: Through identifying and challenging his negative thoughts and conducting behavioral experiments, John's fear of flying significantly decreased. He was able to take flights for work and leisure, reconnect with family members, and feel more in control of his anxiety.

Case Study 3: Overcoming Panic Disorder

BACKGROUND: EMILY IS a 35-year-old woman who has experienced panic attacks for several years. Her panic attacks are sudden episodes of intense fear, accompanied by physical symptoms such as a racing heart, shortness of breath, and dizziness. Her fear of having panic attacks in public places has led to avoidance behaviors, impacting her daily life.

Identifying Negative Thoughts: Emily kept a thought diary and identified several negative thoughts related to panic attacks, such as "I'll have a heart attack," "I'll lose control and go crazy," and "People will think I'm weak."

Challenging Negative Thoughts: With the help of her therapist, Emily used the following questions to challenge her negative thoughts:

- What is the evidence for this thought? "Panic attacks feel intense, but they are not life-threatening. I've had many panic attacks and never had a heart attack."

- What is the evidence against this thought? "Doctors have assured me that my heart is healthy. Panic attacks are a response to anxiety, not a sign of a heart problem."

- Is this thought based on facts or assumptions? "It's an assumption that I'll lose control and go crazy. Panic attacks are a temporary state of heightened anxiety."

- Are there alternative explanations? "My symptoms are caused by the fight-or-flight response, not a medical emergency."

- What is the worst that could happen? "If I have a panic attack in public, it will be uncomfortable, but I can use coping strategies to manage it. People are often more understanding than I think."

- What is the best that could happen? "I might feel anxious but manage the situation effectively and gain confidence."

- What is the most likely outcome? "The most likely outcome is that I'll experience some anxiety but will be able to manage it without losing control."

Behavioral Experiments: Emily designed and conducted several behavioral experiments to test her negative thoughts. For example:

- She practiced relaxation techniques, such as deep breathing and mindfulness, to use during panic attacks.

- She gradually exposed herself to situations she had been avoiding, starting with short trips to the grocery store and gradually increasing the duration and complexity of the situations.

- She predicted that she would have a panic attack and be unable to manage it during a trip to the mall. The actual outcome was that she experienced mild anxiety but used her coping strategies effectively.

Results: Through identifying and challenging her negative thoughts and conducting behavioral experiments, Emily's panic disorder significantly improved. She gained confidence in her ability to manage panic attacks, reduced her avoidance behaviors, and regained control over her daily life.

Additional Cognitive-Behavioral Techniques

IN ADDITION TO CHALLENGING negative thoughts and conducting behavioral experiments, several other cognitive-behavioral techniques can be effective in managing anxiety and phobias. These techniques include relaxation training, problem-solving, and assertiveness training.

Relaxation Training

RELAXATION TRAINING involves learning techniques to reduce physical tension and promote a sense of calm. These techniques can help manage anxiety and prevent the escalation of panic. Some common relaxation techniques include:

1. Deep Breathing: Practice diaphragmatic breathing by inhaling deeply through your nose, allowing your abdomen to expand, and exhaling slowly through your mouth. Repeat this several times to calm your nervous system.

2. Progressive Muscle Relaxation: Tense and relax different muscle groups in your body, starting from your toes and working your way up to your head. This technique can help release physical tension and reduce anxiety.

3. Guided Imagery: Use guided imagery to visualize calming and peaceful scenes. Close your eyes and imagine yourself in a relaxing environment, such as a beach or a forest. Engage your senses by imagining the sights, sounds, and smells of the scene.

4. Mindfulness Meditation: Sit quietly and focus on your breath, observing each inhale and exhale without judgment. When your mind wanders, gently bring your attention back to your breath.

Problem-Solving

PROBLEM-SOLVING IS a cognitive-behavioral technique that helps individuals develop effective strategies for managing stress and anxiety. The problem-solving process involves several steps:

1. Identify the Problem: Clearly define the problem you are facing. Be specific about the situation and what is causing your anxiety.

2. Generate Possible Solutions: Brainstorm a list of potential solutions to the problem. Consider all possible options, even those that may seem less likely to work.

3. Evaluate the Solutions: Assess the pros and cons of each potential solution. Consider the feasibility, potential outcomes, and any potential obstacles.

4. Choose a Solution: Select the solution that seems most effective and feasible. Be realistic about what you can achieve and what resources you have available.

5. Implement the Solution: Put the chosen solution into action. Take practical steps to address the problem and monitor your progress.

6. Evaluate the Outcome: Assess the effectiveness of the solution. If the problem is resolved, consider what you learned from the experience. If the problem persists, consider alternative solutions and repeat the process.

Assertiveness Training

ASSERTIVENESS TRAINING helps individuals develop the skills to communicate their needs, preferences, and boundaries effectively. Assertiveness involves expressing oneself in a clear, respectful, and confident manner. Key components of assertiveness training include:

1. Recognizing Passive, Aggressive, and Assertive Behavior: Understand the differences between passive, aggressive, and assertive communication styles. Passive behavior involves avoiding conflict and not expressing one's needs, while aggressive behavior involves expressing one's needs in a hostile or disrespectful manner. Assertive behavior involves expressing one's needs in a clear, respectful, and confident manner.

2. Using "I" Statements: Practice using "I" statements to express your needs and feelings. For example, "I feel anxious when I'm not informed about changes in the schedule. I would appreciate it if you could let me know in advance."

3. Setting Boundaries: Learn to set clear and respectful boundaries with others. For example, "I need some time to myself to recharge. I'll be available to talk later."

4. Saying No: Practice saying no in a clear and respectful manner. For example, "I'm unable to take on this additional project right now. Thank you for understanding."

5. Active Listening: Develop active listening skills to understand and acknowledge the perspectives of others. Active listening involves paying full attention, nodding, summarizing, and reflecting back what the other person has said.

By incorporating these additional cognitive-behavioral techniques into your routine, you can enhance your ability to manage anxiety and phobias and improve your overall well-being.

Conclusion

Cognitive-behavioral therapy (CBT) is a powerful and effective treatment for anxiety and phobias. By identifying and challenging negative thought patterns, conducting behavioral experiments, and using additional cognitive-behavioral techniques, individuals can reduce their anxiety and improve their quality of life.

Through real-life applications and success stories, we have seen how individuals like Sarah, John, and Emily have successfully used CBT to overcome social anxiety, specific phobias, and panic disorder. Their experiences demonstrate the potential for change and recovery with the right tools and strategies.

Remember, managing anxiety and phobias is a journey that requires patience, persistence, and support. With the right knowledge, resources, and techniques, you can take control of your anxiety and phobias and work toward a future free from excessive fear and avoidance.

Chapter 6: Exposure Therapy

Facing Your Fears Gradually

Exposure therapy is one of the most effective treatments for anxiety disorders and phobias. By gradually facing the objects or situations that provoke fear, individuals can reduce their anxiety over time and learn that their fears are often unfounded. This chapter explains the principles of exposure therapy, provides a step-by-step guide to creating an exposure hierarchy, and offers tips for successful exposure practice.

Explanation of Exposure Therapy

EXPOSURE THERAPY IS a psychological treatment that helps individuals confront their fears in a systematic and controlled manner. The fundamental principle behind exposure therapy is that avoidance of feared objects or situations perpetuates anxiety. By avoiding what we fear, we never give ourselves the opportunity to learn that these situations are not as dangerous as we think.

How Exposure Therapy Works

EXPOSURE THERAPY WORKS through several key mechanisms:

1. Habituation: Habituation refers to the process of becoming accustomed to a stimulus over time. By repeatedly exposing oneself to the feared object or situation, the anxiety response decreases, and the individual becomes less sensitive to the stimulus.

2. Extinction: Extinction involves weakening the association between the feared object or situation and the anxiety response. Over time, the individual learns that the feared outcome does not occur, and the fear response diminishes.

3. Emotional Processing: Exposure therapy helps individuals process and understand their emotions related to the feared object or situation. By confronting their fears, individuals can re-evaluate their beliefs and develop more accurate and balanced perspectives.

4. Self-Efficacy: Exposure therapy enhances self-efficacy, or the belief in one's ability to cope with fear and anxiety. By successfully facing their fears, individuals gain confidence in their ability to handle challenging situations.

Types of Exposure Therapy

THERE ARE SEVERAL TYPES of exposure therapy, each tailored to the specific needs and preferences of the individual. The main types of exposure therapy include:

1. In Vivo Exposure: In vivo exposure involves facing the feared object or situation in real life. For example, someone with a fear of flying might gradually work up to taking a flight.

2. Imaginal Exposure: Imaginal exposure involves vividly imagining the feared object or situation. This type of exposure is useful for fears that are not easily encountered in real life, such as traumatic memories or irrational fears.

3. Virtual Reality Exposure: Virtual reality (VR) exposure uses computer-generated environments to simulate feared situations. VR exposure is particularly useful for phobias such as fear of heights or public speaking, where real-life exposure may be difficult to arrange.

4. Interoceptive Exposure: Interoceptive exposure involves deliberately inducing physical sensations that are feared, such as a racing heart or shortness of breath. This type of exposure is commonly used for panic disorder to help individuals become more comfortable with the sensations of anxiety.

Step-by-Step Guide to Creating an Exposure Hierarchy

CREATING AN EXPOSURE hierarchy is a critical component of exposure therapy. An exposure hierarchy is a list of feared situations or objects ranked in order of difficulty. The hierarchy serves as a roadmap for exposure exercises, starting with less challenging situations and gradually progressing to more difficult ones.

Step 1: Identify Your Fears

THE FIRST STEP IN CREATING an exposure hierarchy is to identify your specific fears. Consider the situations, objects, or activities that provoke anxiety or avoidance. Be as detailed as possible in describing these fears.

For example, if you have a fear of public speaking, your list might include:

- Speaking up in a small meeting.

- Giving a presentation to a small group of colleagues.

- Speaking in a large meeting.

- Giving a speech at a family gathering.

- Presenting at a conference.

Step 2: Rate the Level of Anxiety

NEXT, RATE THE LEVEL of anxiety associated with each situation on your list. Use a scale from 0 to 10, where 0 represents no anxiety and 10 represents extreme anxiety. This rating will help you prioritize the items on your hierarchy.

Using the public speaking example, your ratings might look like this:

- Speaking up in a small meeting: 3

- Giving a presentation to a small group of colleagues: 5

- Speaking in a large meeting: 6

- Giving a speech at a family gathering: 8

- Presenting at a conference: 10

Step 3: Rank the Items in Order

ONCE YOU HAVE RATED the level of anxiety for each item, rank the items in order from least to most anxiety-provoking. This ranking will serve as your exposure hierarchy.

For example:

1. Speaking up in a small meeting: 3

2. Giving a presentation to a small group of colleagues: 5

3. Speaking in a large meeting: 6

4. Giving a speech at a family gathering: 8

5. Presenting at a conference: 10

Step 4: Develop Exposure Exercises

DEVELOP SPECIFIC EXPOSURE exercises for each item on your hierarchy. These exercises should involve gradually and systematically facing the feared situation. Start with the least anxiety-provoking item and work your way up the hierarchy.

For example:

- **Speaking up in a small meeting**:

- Attend a small meeting and practice speaking up once.

- Gradually increase the number of times you speak up in subsequent meetings.

- Giving a presentation to a small group of colleagues:

- Practice your presentation at home.

- Give your presentation to a trusted friend or family member.

- Give your presentation to a small group of colleagues.

- Speaking in a large meeting:

- Attend a large meeting and practice speaking up once.

- Gradually increase the number of times you speak up in subsequent meetings.

- Giving a speech at a family gathering:

- Practice your speech at home.

- Give your speech to a small group of family members.

- Give your speech at a family gathering.

- Presenting at a conference:

- Practice your presentation at home.

- Give your presentation to a small group of colleagues or friends.

- Present at a smaller, less formal event.

- Present at the conference.

Tips for Successful Exposure Practice

EXPOSURE THERAPY CAN be challenging, but there are several strategies that can help you practice exposure exercises successfully and achieve the best results.

Tip 1: Start Small and Progress Gradually

ONE OF THE KEY PRINCIPLES of exposure therapy is to start with less anxiety-provoking situations and gradually progress to more challenging ones. This gradual approach helps build confidence and reduce anxiety over time. It is important not to rush the process and to take small, manageable steps.

Tip 2: Set Realistic Goals

SET REALISTIC AND ACHIEVABLE goals for your exposure exercises. Each step on your hierarchy should be challenging but not overwhelming. It is important to recognize that progress may be gradual, and setbacks are a normal part of the process. Celebrate your successes and be patient with yourself.

Tip 3: Practice Regularly

REGULAR PRACTICE IS essential for the success of exposure therapy. Consistent and repeated exposure to feared situations helps reduce anxiety and reinforce learning. Schedule regular exposure exercises and commit to practicing them, even if it feels uncomfortable.

Tip 4: Use Relaxation Techniques

INCORPORATE RELAXATION techniques, such as deep breathing, progressive muscle relaxation, and mindfulness meditation, into your exposure practice. These techniques can help manage anxiety and make the exposure exercises more manageable. Practice relaxation techniques before, during, and after exposure exercises.

Tip 5: Challenge Negative Thoughts

DURING EXPOSURE EXERCISES, you may experience negative thoughts and cognitive distortions. Use cognitive-behavioral techniques to challenge and reframe these thoughts. Remind yourself of the evidence against your fears and focus on more balanced and realistic perspectives.

Tip 6: Use a Support System

HAVING A SUPPORT SYSTEM can provide encouragement and motivation during exposure therapy. Share your goals and progress with trusted friends, family members, or a therapist. They can offer support, feedback, and reinforcement as you work through your exposure hierarchy.

Tip 7: Record Your Progress

KEEP A JOURNAL OR LOG to record your exposure exercises, including the situations you faced, your anxiety levels, and your observations. Tracking your progress can help you see the improvements over time and reinforce your accomplishments.

Tip 8: Be Patient and Persistent

EXPOSURE THERAPY CAN be a challenging and gradual process. It is important to be patient with yourself and to persist even when it feels difficult. Recognize that setbacks and fluctuations in anxiety levels are normal. Stay committed to your goals and continue practicing exposure exercises regularly.

Tip 9: Seek Professional Guidance

IF YOU FIND IT DIFFICULT to practice exposure therapy on your own or if your anxiety is severe, consider seeking guidance from a mental health professional. A therapist can help you develop a tailored exposure hierarchy, provide support and encouragement, and address any challenges that arise during the process.

Real-Life Applications and Success Stories

TO ILLUSTRATE THE EFFECTIVENESS of exposure therapy, here are real-life applications and success stories of individuals who have used exposure therapy to overcome their fears and anxiety.

Case Study 1: Overcoming a Specific Phobia (Fear of Heights)

BACKGROUND: JESSICA is a 28-year-old woman with a severe fear of heights (acrophobia). Her phobia began during childhood after a traumatic experience on a high bridge. Her fear of heights has led to significant avoidance behaviors, such as avoiding tall buildings, bridges, and other elevated places.

Creating an Exposure Hierarchy: With the help of her therapist, Jessica created an exposure hierarchy for her fear of heights. The hierarchy included the following items:

1. Looking at pictures of tall buildings: 3

2. Watching videos of people on high places: 4

3. Standing on a small step stool: 5

4. Going up one floor in a building and looking out the window: 6

5. Going to a rooftop terrace on a low-rise building: 7

6. Walking on a pedestrian bridge: 8

7. Going up to a high floor in a skyscraper: 9

8. Visiting an observation deck on a tall building: 10

Exposure Exercises: Jessica gradually worked through her exposure hierarchy with the support of her therapist:

- She started by looking at pictures of tall buildings and watching videos of people on high places until her anxiety decreased.

- She then stood on a small step stool at home, gradually increasing the duration until she felt more comfortable.

- She visited a low-rise building and looked out the window from the first floor, gradually progressing to higher floors.

- She practiced walking on a pedestrian bridge, first with her therapist and later on her own.

- She gradually worked up to visiting an observation deck on a tall building, using relaxation techniques and cognitive-behavioral strategies to manage her anxiety.

Results: Through consistent exposure practice, Jessica's fear of heights significantly decreased. She gained confidence in her ability to handle elevated places and reduced her avoidance behaviors. She was able to visit tall buildings and enjoy activities that she had previously avoided.

Case Study 2: Overcoming Social Anxiety

BACKGROUND: MARK IS a 35-year-old man with social anxiety disorder. His fear of social interactions began in adolescence and has led to significant avoidance behaviors, such as avoiding parties, meetings, and public speaking. His social anxiety has impacted his personal and professional life.

Creating an Exposure Hierarchy: With the help of his therapist, Mark created an exposure hierarchy for his social anxiety. The hierarchy included the following items:

1. Making small talk with a cashier: 3

2. Introducing himself to a new colleague: 4

3. Attending a small social gathering: 5

4. Speaking up in a small meeting: 6

5. Giving a presentation to a small group of colleagues: 7

6. Attending a large social event: 8

7. Giving a speech at a family gathering: 9

8. Presenting at a conference: 10

Exposure Exercises: Mark gradually worked through his exposure hierarchy with the support of his therapist:

- He started by making small talk with a cashier and introducing himself to new colleagues until his anxiety decreased.

- He then attended small social gatherings and practiced speaking up in meetings.

- He gradually worked up to giving presentations to colleagues and attending large social events.

- He practiced giving speeches at family gatherings and eventually presented at a conference, using relaxation techniques and cognitive-behavioral strategies to manage his anxiety.

Results: Through consistent exposure practice, Mark's social anxiety significantly decreased. He gained confidence in his ability to handle social interactions and reduced his avoidance behaviors. He was able to participate in social and professional activities that he had previously avoided.

Case Study 3: Overcoming Panic Disorder with Agoraphobia

BACKGROUND: EMILY IS a 40-year-old woman with panic disorder and agoraphobia. Her fear of having panic attacks in public places has led to significant avoidance behaviors, such as avoiding malls, restaurants, and public transportation. Her agoraphobia has impacted her daily life and independence.

Creating an Exposure Hierarchy: With the help of her therapist, Emily created an exposure hierarchy for her agoraphobia. The hierarchy included the following items:

1. Walking to a nearby park: 3

2. Visiting a small grocery store: 4

3. Taking a short bus ride: 5

4. Eating at a quiet restaurant: 6

5. Going to a small shopping mall: 7

6. Taking a longer bus ride: 8

7. Visiting a large shopping mall: 9

8. Taking a train ride to a nearby city: 10

Exposure Exercises: Emily gradually worked through her exposure hierarchy with the support of her therapist:

- She started by walking to a nearby park and visiting a small grocery store until her anxiety decreased.

- She then took short bus rides and practiced eating at quiet restaurants.

- She gradually worked up to visiting small shopping malls and taking longer bus rides.

- She practiced visiting large shopping malls and eventually took a train ride to a nearby city, using relaxation techniques and cognitive-behavioral strategies to manage her anxiety.

Results: Through consistent exposure practice, Emily's panic disorder and agoraphobia significantly improved. She gained confidence in her ability to handle public places and reduced her avoidance behaviors. She was able to regain her independence and participate in activities that she had previously avoided.

Conclusion

Exposure therapy is a powerful and effective treatment for anxiety disorders and phobias. By gradually facing feared situations in a systematic and controlled manner, individuals can reduce their anxiety and learn that their fears are often unfounded.

Creating an exposure hierarchy is a critical component of exposure therapy, providing a structured roadmap for exposure exercises. Starting with less anxiety-provoking situations and gradually progressing to more challenging ones helps build confidence and reduce anxiety over time.

Successful exposure practice requires setting realistic goals, practicing regularly, using relaxation techniques, challenging negative thoughts, and seeking support from trusted individuals or a therapist. By following these tips and strategies, individuals can achieve significant improvements in their anxiety and phobias.

Real-life applications and success stories, such as those of Jessica, Mark, and Emily, demonstrate the potential for change and recovery with exposure therapy. Their experiences highlight the effectiveness of facing fears gradually and the positive impact it can have on one's quality of life.

Remember, managing anxiety and phobias is a journey that requires patience, persistence, and support. With the right knowledge, resources, and techniques, you can take control of your anxiety and phobias and work toward a future free from excessive fear and avoidance.

Chapter 7: Mindfulness and Relaxation Techniques

Staying Present and Calm

Mindfulness and relaxation techniques are powerful tools for managing anxiety and stress. By staying present and calm, individuals can reduce their anxiety, improve their overall well-being, and enhance their quality of life. This chapter introduces mindfulness and its benefits, provides detailed instructions for breathing exercises, meditation, and progressive muscle relaxation, and offers practical tips for incorporating mindfulness into daily life.

Introduction to Mindfulness and Its Benefits

MINDFULNESS IS THE practice of paying attention to the present moment without judgment. It involves being fully aware of your thoughts, feelings, bodily sensations, and the surrounding environment. Mindfulness is rooted in ancient meditation practices, particularly those from Buddhist traditions, but it has been widely adopted in Western psychology for its mental health benefits.

The Core Principles of Mindfulness

MINDFULNESS IS BASED on several core principles that guide its practice:

1. Present Moment Awareness: Mindfulness involves focusing on the here and now, rather than dwelling on the past or worrying about the future. This present moment awareness helps individuals experience life more fully and reduces rumination and anxiety.

2. Non-Judgment: Practicing mindfulness involves observing your thoughts and feelings without labeling them as good or bad. This non-judgmental

approach fosters acceptance and self-compassion, which can alleviate stress and improve emotional well-being.

3. Acceptance: Mindfulness encourages accepting things as they are, rather than trying to change or control them. Acceptance allows individuals to let go of resistance and find peace in the present moment.

4. Curiosity: Mindfulness involves approaching each moment with curiosity and openness, as if experiencing it for the first time. This curious attitude helps individuals stay engaged and interested in their experiences.

The Benefits of Mindfulness

RESEARCH HAS SHOWN that mindfulness offers a wide range of benefits for mental and physical health. Some of the key benefits include:

1. Reducing Anxiety and Stress: Mindfulness practices have been shown to reduce symptoms of anxiety and stress by promoting relaxation, enhancing emotional regulation, and decreasing rumination.

2. Improving Emotional Well-Being: Mindfulness fosters greater self-awareness and acceptance, which can lead to improved emotional well-being, increased resilience, and a greater sense of inner peace.

3. Enhancing Focus and Concentration: Mindfulness training improves attention and concentration by encouraging individuals to focus on the present moment and reduce distractions.

4. Improving Sleep: Mindfulness practices can improve sleep quality by promoting relaxation and reducing the mental chatter that can interfere with falling and staying asleep.

5. Enhancing Physical Health: Mindfulness has been linked to various physical health benefits, including lower blood pressure, improved immune function, and reduced symptoms of chronic pain.

6. Improving Relationships: Mindfulness enhances empathy, communication, and emotional regulation, which can improve relationships and increase social connectedness.

Breathing Exercises, Meditation, and Progressive Muscle Relaxation

MINDFULNESS AND RELAXATION techniques encompass a variety of practices, including breathing exercises, meditation, and progressive muscle relaxation. These techniques can be used individually or in combination to promote relaxation and reduce anxiety.

Breathing Exercises

BREATHING EXERCISES are a simple yet effective way to promote relaxation and reduce anxiety. By focusing on your breath, you can activate the body's relaxation response and calm the mind.

Diaphragmatic Breathing (also known as abdominal or belly breathing) involves deep, slow breaths that engage the diaphragm. This type of breathing helps activate the parasympathetic nervous system, which promotes relaxation.

Instructions for Diaphragmatic Breathing:

1. Find a comfortable position, either sitting or lying down.

2. Place one hand on your chest and the other hand on your abdomen.

3. Inhale deeply through your nose, allowing your abdomen to expand as you fill your lungs with air. Your chest should remain relatively still.

4. Exhale slowly and completely through your mouth, allowing your abdomen to fall.

5. Continue breathing deeply and slowly, focusing on the rise and fall of your abdomen with each breath.

6. Practice this exercise for 5-10 minutes, or longer if desired.

4-7-8 Breathing is another effective breathing exercise that can promote relaxation and reduce anxiety. It involves a specific pattern of inhaling, holding the breath, and exhaling.

Instructions for 4-7-8 Breathing:

1. Sit or lie down in a comfortable position.

2. Close your eyes and take a deep breath in through your nose for a count of 4.

3. Hold your breath for a count of 7.

4. Exhale slowly and completely through your mouth for a count of 8.

5. Repeat this cycle 4-8 times, or until you feel more relaxed.

Box Breathing (also known as square breathing) is a simple technique that involves breathing in a pattern of equal counts.

Instructions for Box Breathing:

1. Sit in a comfortable position with your back straight and feet flat on the floor.

2. Inhale slowly and deeply through your nose for a count of 4.

3. Hold your breath for a count of 4.

4. Exhale slowly and completely through your mouth for a count of 4.

5. Hold your breath again for a count of 4.

6. Repeat this cycle for 5-10 minutes, or until you feel more relaxed.

Meditation

Meditation is a practice that involves focusing the mind and eliminating distractions to achieve a state of deep relaxation and heightened awareness. There are many forms of meditation, each with its own techniques and benefits.

Mindfulness Meditation involves paying attention to the present moment without judgment. This practice can help reduce anxiety, improve emotional regulation, and enhance overall well-being.

Instructions for Mindfulness Meditation:

1. Find a quiet place where you can sit comfortably without distractions.

2. Sit in a comfortable position with your back straight and hands resting on your lap.

3. Close your eyes and take a few deep breaths to relax.

4. Bring your attention to your breath, noticing the sensation of each inhale and exhale.

5. If your mind wanders, gently bring your attention back to your breath without judgment.

6. Continue focusing on your breath for 5-10 minutes, or longer if desired.

Loving-Kindness Meditation (also known as Metta meditation) involves cultivating feelings of compassion and love for oneself and others. This practice can enhance emotional well-being and improve relationships.

Instructions for Loving-Kindness Meditation:

1. Find a quiet place where you can sit comfortably without distractions.

2. Sit in a comfortable position with your back straight and hands resting on your lap.

3. Close your eyes and take a few deep breaths to relax.

4. Begin by focusing on yourself and silently repeating the following phrases:

- May I be happy.

- May I be healthy.

- May I be safe.

- May I live with ease.

5. Next, think of someone you love and care about. Silently repeat the phrases for them:

- May you be happy.

- May you be healthy.

- May you be safe.

- May you live with ease.

6. Continue extending these phrases to others, including friends, family, acquaintances, and even those with whom you have conflicts.

7. Conclude the meditation by extending loving-kindness to all beings:

- May all beings be happy.

- May all beings be healthy.

- May all beings be safe.

- May all beings live with ease.

Body Scan Meditation involves paying attention to different parts of the body and noticing any sensations or tension. This practice can promote relaxation and increase body awareness.

Instructions for Body Scan Meditation:

1. Find a quiet place where you can lie down comfortably without distractions.

2. Lie down on your back with your arms resting at your sides and your legs slightly apart.

3. Close your eyes and take a few deep breaths to relax.

4. Begin by bringing your attention to your toes. Notice any sensations or tension in this area.

5. Gradually move your attention up your body, focusing on each part in turn (e.g., feet, ankles, calves, knees, thighs, hips, abdomen, chest, shoulders, arms, hands, neck, and head).

6. As you focus on each part of your body, notice any sensations, tension, or areas of relaxation.

7. If you notice any tension, imagine releasing it with each exhale.

8. Continue the body scan until you have focused on each part of your body.

Guided Imagery involves using the power of imagination to create calming and peaceful mental images. This practice can help reduce anxiety and promote relaxation.

Instructions for Guided Imagery:

1. Find a quiet place where you can sit or lie down comfortably without distractions.

2. Close your eyes and take a few deep breaths to relax.

3. Imagine yourself in a peaceful and calming place, such as a beach, forest, or garden.

4. Engage your senses by imagining the sights, sounds, smells, and sensations of this place.

5. Spend a few minutes exploring and enjoying this peaceful place in your mind.

6. When you are ready, slowly bring your attention back to the present moment and open your eyes.

Progressive Muscle Relaxation

PROGRESSIVE MUSCLE relaxation (PMR) is a technique that involves tensing and relaxing different muscle groups in the body. This practice can help release physical tension and promote relaxation.

Instructions for Progressive Muscle Relaxation:

1. Find a quiet place where you can sit or lie down comfortably without distractions.

2. Close your eyes and take a few deep breaths to relax.

3. Begin by focusing on your toes. Tense the muscles in your toes for 5-10 seconds, then release and relax for 15-20 seconds.

4. Move to the next muscle group (e.g., feet, calves, thighs, hips, abdomen, chest, shoulders, arms, hands, neck, and head), tensing and relaxing each group in turn.

5. As you tense each muscle group, focus on the sensation of tension. As you relax each group, focus on the sensation of release and relaxation.

6. Continue the process until you have tensed and relaxed all muscle groups in your body.

Incorporating Mindfulness into Daily Life

INCORPORATING MINDFULNESS into your daily life can help you stay present and calm, reduce anxiety, and improve overall well-being. Here are some practical tips for integrating mindfulness into your daily routine:

Morning Routine

START YOUR DAY WITH mindfulness to set a positive tone for the rest of the day.

Tips for a Mindful Morning Routine:

1. Mindful Breathing: Begin your day with a few minutes of mindful breathing. Sit quietly and focus on your breath, noticing the sensation of each inhale and exhale.

2. Morning Stretch: Incorporate a few gentle stretches or yoga poses into your morning routine. Focus on the sensations in your body and your breath as you stretch.

3. Mindful Eating: Eat your breakfast mindfully by paying attention to the taste, texture, and aroma of your food. Eat slowly and savor each bite.

Daily Activities

BRING MINDFULNESS TO your daily activities to stay present and reduce stress.

Tips for Mindful Daily Activities:

1. Mindful Walking: Practice mindful walking by paying attention to the sensation of your feet touching the ground, the movement of your body, and the sights and sounds around you.

2. Mindful Listening: Practice mindful listening by giving your full attention to the person speaking. Focus on their words, tone of voice, and body language without interrupting or judging.

3. Mindful Cleaning: Bring mindfulness to household chores, such as washing dishes or cleaning. Focus on the sensations, movements, and sounds of the task.

Work and Study

INCORPORATE MINDFULNESS into your work or study routine to enhance focus and reduce stress.

Tips for Mindful Work and Study:

1. Mindful Breaks: Take regular mindful breaks throughout your work or study day. Spend a few minutes focusing on your breath or doing a short mindfulness exercise.

2. Mindful Transitions: Practice mindfulness during transitions between tasks or meetings. Take a few deep breaths and bring your attention to the present moment.

3. Mindful Focus: When working or studying, practice single-tasking by focusing on one task at a time. Avoid multitasking and bring your full attention to the task at hand.

Evening Routine

END YOUR DAY WITH MINDFULNESS to promote relaxation and improve sleep quality.

Tips for a Mindful Evening Routine:

1. Mindful Reflection: Spend a few minutes reflecting on your day. Focus on the positive moments and any challenges you faced. Practice gratitude by acknowledging things you are thankful for.

2. Mindful Relaxation: Practice a relaxation technique, such as diaphragmatic breathing, progressive muscle relaxation, or guided imagery, to unwind before bed.

3. Mindful Reading: If you enjoy reading before bed, choose a calming and enjoyable book. Read mindfully by focusing on the words and the experience of reading.

Mindful Technology Use

USE TECHNOLOGY MINDFULLY to reduce distractions and enhance your well-being.

Tips for Mindful Technology Use:

1. Mindful Notifications: Turn off non-essential notifications on your devices to reduce distractions. Check your messages and emails at designated times rather than constantly.

2. Mindful Social Media: Use social media mindfully by setting time limits and being intentional about your usage. Focus on positive and meaningful interactions rather than mindless scrolling.

3. Mindful Screen Time: Take regular breaks from screens to rest your eyes and mind. Practice the 20-20-20 rule: every 20 minutes, look at something 20 feet away for at least 20 seconds.

Real-Life Applications and Success Stories

TO ILLUSTRATE THE EFFECTIVENESS of mindfulness and relaxation techniques, here are real-life applications and success stories of individuals who have used these practices to manage anxiety and improve their overall well-being.

Case Study 1: Reducing Work-Related Stress with Mindfulness

BACKGROUND: LAURA IS a 40-year-old marketing executive who has been experiencing high levels of work-related stress. Her demanding job involves long hours, tight deadlines, and frequent travel. The stress has been affecting her sleep, mood, and overall health.

Mindfulness Practice: Laura decided to incorporate mindfulness into her daily routine to manage her stress. She started with a morning mindfulness practice, which included 10 minutes of diaphragmatic breathing and a few gentle stretches. Throughout her workday, she took regular mindful breaks, spending a few minutes focusing on her breath or doing a short mindfulness exercise. She also practiced mindful transitions between tasks and meetings by taking a few deep breaths and bringing her attention to the present moment.

Results: Over time, Laura noticed a significant reduction in her stress levels. She felt more focused and calm during her workday and found it easier to manage tight deadlines and high-pressure situations. Her sleep improved, and she felt more energized and positive. By incorporating mindfulness into her daily routine, Laura was able to reduce her work-related stress and enhance her overall well-being.

Case Study 2: Managing Anxiety with Progressive Muscle Relaxation

BACKGROUND: JAMES IS a 30-year-old software developer who has been struggling with anxiety for several years. His anxiety manifests as physical tension, particularly in his neck and shoulders, and he often experiences headaches and muscle pain.

Relaxation Practice: James decided to try progressive muscle relaxation (PMR) to manage his anxiety and physical tension. He practiced PMR every evening before bed, following the instructions to tense and relax different muscle groups in his body. He also incorporated diaphragmatic breathing into his PMR practice to enhance relaxation.

Results: After a few weeks of regular PMR practice, James noticed a significant reduction in his physical tension and anxiety levels. His headaches and muscle pain decreased, and he felt more relaxed and at ease. By incorporating PMR into his routine, James was able to manage his anxiety more effectively and improve his physical health.

Case Study 3: Improving Emotional Well-Being with Loving-Kindness Meditation

BACKGROUND: SARAH IS a 35-year-old teacher who has been experiencing feelings of loneliness and low self-esteem. She often criticizes herself and finds it difficult to connect with others.

Mindfulness Practice: Sarah decided to try loving-kindness meditation to improve her emotional well-being and enhance her relationships. She practiced loving-kindness meditation for 10-15 minutes every morning, following the instructions to extend feelings of compassion and love to herself and others.

Results: After a few weeks of regular loving-kindness meditation practice, Sarah noticed a significant improvement in her emotional well-being. She felt more compassionate and accepting of herself and others. Her self-esteem increased, and she found it easier to connect with others and build positive relationships. By incorporating loving-kindness meditation into her routine,

Sarah was able to improve her emotional well-being and enhance her social connections.

Conclusion

Mindfulness and relaxation techniques are powerful tools for managing anxiety and stress. By staying present and calm, individuals can reduce their anxiety, improve their overall well-being, and enhance their quality of life.

Breathing exercises, meditation, and progressive muscle relaxation are effective practices that promote relaxation and reduce anxiety. Incorporating these techniques into your daily routine can help you stay present, reduce stress, and improve your overall well-being.

Real-life applications and success stories, such as those of Laura, James, and Sarah, demonstrate the potential for change and recovery with mindfulness and relaxation practices. Their experiences highlight the effectiveness of staying present and calm and the positive impact it can have on one's quality of life.

Remember, managing anxiety and stress is a journey that requires patience, persistence, and support. With the right knowledge, resources, and techniques, you can take control of your anxiety and stress and work toward a future free from excessive fear and tension.

Chapter 8: Lifestyle Changes for Anxiety Management

Building a Healthier Routine

Lifestyle changes can play a crucial role in managing anxiety. By making intentional choices about diet, exercise, sleep, self-care, and boundaries, individuals can create a healthier routine that supports their mental well-being. This chapter explores the impact of diet, exercise, and sleep on anxiety, provides guidance on developing a balanced lifestyle, and emphasizes the importance of self-care and boundaries.

The Impact of Diet, Exercise, and Sleep on Anxiety

DIET

Diet plays a significant role in mental health, and certain foods and eating habits can either alleviate or exacerbate anxiety. Understanding the connection between diet and anxiety can help individuals make informed choices that support their mental well-being.

Nutrient-Rich Foods

A BALANCED DIET RICH in essential nutrients can support brain health and reduce anxiety. Some key nutrients and their sources include:

1. Omega-3 Fatty Acids: Found in fatty fish (such as salmon, mackerel, and sardines), flaxseeds, chia seeds, and walnuts, omega-3 fatty acids have anti-inflammatory properties and support brain function. Studies have shown that omega-3s can reduce symptoms of anxiety and depression.

2. Magnesium: Magnesium is involved in many biochemical reactions in the body, including those related to stress and anxiety. Foods rich in magnesium

include leafy green vegetables (such as spinach and kale), nuts, seeds, whole grains, and legumes.

3. Vitamin D: Vitamin D is essential for brain health and mood regulation. Sunlight exposure is a primary source of vitamin D, but it can also be obtained from foods such as fatty fish, fortified dairy products, and egg yolks. Low levels of vitamin D have been linked to increased anxiety and depression.

4. B Vitamins: B vitamins, particularly B6, B12, and folate, play a crucial role in brain function and the production of neurotransmitters. Foods rich in B vitamins include whole grains, eggs, lean meats, legumes, and leafy green vegetables.

5. Probiotics: The gut-brain connection highlights the importance of gut health in mental well-being. Probiotics, found in fermented foods such as yogurt, kefir, sauerkraut, and kimchi, can support a healthy gut microbiome and reduce anxiety.

Avoiding Anxiety-Provoking Foods

CERTAIN FOODS AND SUBSTANCES can exacerbate anxiety and should be consumed in moderation or avoided:

1. Caffeine: Caffeine is a stimulant that can increase heart rate and anxiety levels. Reducing or eliminating caffeine intake from coffee, tea, energy drinks, and certain medications can help manage anxiety.

2. Sugar: High sugar intake can lead to blood sugar spikes and crashes, which can affect mood and anxiety levels. Limiting the consumption of sugary foods and beverages can promote more stable blood sugar levels and reduce anxiety.

3. Alcohol: While alcohol may initially seem to reduce anxiety, it can disrupt sleep and negatively impact mood. Reducing or avoiding alcohol can support better mental health.

4. Processed Foods: Processed foods often contain additives, preservatives, and unhealthy fats that can negatively affect brain function and mood. Choosing whole, unprocessed foods can support overall health and reduce anxiety.

Mindful Eating

MINDFUL EATING INVOLVES paying attention to the experience of eating and enjoying food without distractions. This practice can promote a healthier relationship with food and reduce anxiety related to eating.

Tips for Mindful Eating:

1. Eat Slowly: Take your time to chew and savor each bite. Eating slowly can improve digestion and help you recognize when you are full.

2. Focus on Your Food: Avoid distractions such as watching TV or using your phone while eating. Focus on the taste, texture, and aroma of your food.

3. Listen to Your Body: Pay attention to your body's hunger and fullness cues. Eat when you are hungry and stop when you are satisfied.

4. Enjoy Your Meals: Take the time to prepare and enjoy nutritious meals. Eating in a relaxed and pleasant environment can enhance the experience.

Exercise

Regular physical activity is one of the most effective ways to manage anxiety. Exercise releases endorphins, which are natural mood lifters, and helps reduce stress hormones such as cortisol. Incorporating exercise into your routine can have profound benefits for mental health.

Types of Exercise

DIFFERENT TYPES OF exercise offer various benefits for anxiety management. Here are some effective forms of exercise to consider:

1. Aerobic Exercise: Activities such as running, cycling, swimming, and dancing increase heart rate and improve cardiovascular health. Aerobic exercise

has been shown to reduce anxiety and improve mood by releasing endorphins and promoting relaxation.

2. Strength Training: Strength training exercises, such as weightlifting and resistance training, build muscle and improve overall fitness. Strength training can enhance self-esteem and provide a sense of accomplishment, which can reduce anxiety.

3. Yoga: Yoga combines physical postures, breathing exercises, and meditation to promote relaxation and reduce anxiety. Regular yoga practice can improve flexibility, strength, and mental clarity.

4. Mindful Movement: Activities such as tai chi and qigong involve slow, deliberate movements and focus on breath and mindfulness. These practices can reduce anxiety and promote a sense of calm and balance.

5. Outdoor Activities: Spending time in nature and engaging in outdoor activities, such as hiking, gardening, or walking, can reduce anxiety and improve mood. Nature exposure has been shown to have a calming effect on the mind.

Creating an Exercise Routine

DEVELOPING A CONSISTENT exercise routine can help you manage anxiety effectively. Here are some tips for creating an exercise routine that works for you:

1. Set Realistic Goals: Start with achievable goals and gradually increase the intensity and duration of your exercise. Setting realistic goals can help you stay motivated and avoid burnout.

2. Find Activities You Enjoy: Choose activities that you find enjoyable and fun. Enjoying your exercise routine can make it easier to stick with it.

3. Schedule Regular Exercise: Incorporate exercise into your daily or weekly schedule. Consistency is key to reaping the benefits of physical activity.

4. Mix It Up: Vary your exercise routine to keep it interesting and engaging. Trying different activities can prevent boredom and challenge your body in new ways.

5. Listen to Your Body: Pay attention to your body's signals and avoid overexertion. Rest and recovery are important components of a balanced exercise routine.

Sleep

Sleep is essential for overall health and well-being, and it plays a critical role in managing anxiety. Poor sleep quality or insufficient sleep can exacerbate anxiety and affect mood, cognitive function, and physical health.

The Importance of Sleep

ADEQUATE AND RESTFUL sleep supports mental and physical health in several ways:

1. Emotional Regulation: Sleep helps regulate emotions and reduce irritability and mood swings. A good night's sleep can enhance emotional resilience and improve stress management.

2. Cognitive Function: Sleep is essential for cognitive processes such as memory consolidation, problem-solving, and decision-making. Poor sleep can impair cognitive function and increase anxiety.

3. Physical Health: Sleep supports the body's healing and repair processes, boosts the immune system, and regulates hormones. Chronic sleep deprivation can lead to various health issues, including increased anxiety.

Tips for Improving Sleep Quality

IMPROVING SLEEP QUALITY can significantly reduce anxiety and enhance overall well-being. Here are some tips for getting better sleep:

1. Establish a Sleep Routine: Create a consistent sleep schedule by going to bed and waking up at the same time every day, even on weekends. A regular sleep routine can help regulate your body's internal clock.

2. Create a Relaxing Bedtime Routine: Develop a calming bedtime routine to signal to your body that it's time to wind down. Activities such as reading, taking a warm bath, or practicing relaxation exercises can promote relaxation and prepare you for sleep.

3. Limit Screen Time: Reduce exposure to screens (such as phones, tablets, and computers) at least an hour before bedtime. The blue light emitted by screens can interfere with the production of melatonin, a hormone that regulates sleep.

4. Create a Comfortable Sleep Environment: Make your bedroom conducive to sleep by keeping it cool, dark, and quiet. Invest in a comfortable mattress and pillows, and remove any distractions that may interfere with sleep.

5. Limit Caffeine and Alcohol: Avoid consuming caffeine and alcohol in the hours leading up to bedtime. Both substances can disrupt sleep and affect sleep quality.

6. Practice Relaxation Techniques: Incorporate relaxation techniques, such as deep breathing, progressive muscle relaxation, or guided imagery, into your bedtime routine to promote relaxation and reduce anxiety.

Developing a Balanced Lifestyle

IN ADDITION TO DIET, exercise, and sleep, developing a balanced lifestyle involves making intentional choices that support overall well-being. A balanced lifestyle includes a harmonious blend of work, leisure, social connections, and self-care.

Work-Life Balance

ACHIEVING A HEALTHY work-life balance is essential for managing anxiety and preventing burnout. Here are some strategies for maintaining a healthy balance between work and personal life:

1. Set Boundaries: Establish clear boundaries between work and personal time. Avoid bringing work home and designate specific times for work-related tasks.

2. Prioritize Tasks: Focus on prioritizing tasks and managing your time effectively. Break larger tasks into smaller, manageable steps and set realistic deadlines.

3. Take Breaks: Schedule regular breaks throughout your workday to rest and recharge. Short breaks can improve focus and productivity.

4. Unplug: Disconnect from work-related technology outside of work hours. Avoid checking emails or taking work calls during your personal time.

5. Delegate: Delegate tasks and responsibilities when possible to avoid overloading yourself. Seek support from colleagues or team members when needed.

Leisure and Recreation

ENGAGING IN LEISURE and recreational activities is important for relaxation and enjoyment. Here are some tips for incorporating leisure into your routine:

1. Pursue Hobbies: Make time for hobbies and activities that you enjoy. Whether it's reading, painting, gardening, or playing a musical instrument, engaging in enjoyable activities can reduce stress and enhance well-being.

2. Explore New Interests: Try new activities or interests to keep things fresh and exciting. Exploring new hobbies can provide a sense of accomplishment and fulfillment.

3. Socialize: Spend time with friends and family to build social connections and support networks. Socializing can improve mood and reduce feelings of isolation.

4. Plan Regular Outings: Plan regular outings or activities, such as picnics, hikes, or visits to museums. Getting out and exploring new places can provide a mental break and promote relaxation.

Social Connections

STRONG SOCIAL CONNECTIONS are vital for mental health and well-being. Here are some strategies for building and maintaining meaningful relationships:

1. Nurture Existing Relationships: Invest time and effort in maintaining relationships with friends and family. Regular communication and spending quality time together can strengthen bonds.

2. Seek Support: Reach out to trusted friends, family members, or support groups when you need emotional support. Sharing your thoughts and feelings can provide relief and validation.

3. Build New Connections: Join clubs, groups, or organizations that align with your interests. Building new connections can expand your social network and provide opportunities for social interaction.

4. Practice Active Listening: Show genuine interest in others by practicing active listening. Pay attention, ask questions, and engage in meaningful conversations.

The Importance of Self-Care and Boundaries

SELF-CARE INVOLVES taking intentional actions to care for your physical, emotional, and mental well-being. Setting boundaries is an essential aspect of self-care, as it helps protect your energy and maintain balance in your life.

Self-Care Practices

INCORPORATING SELF-care practices into your routine can help you manage anxiety and enhance overall well-being. Here are some self-care practices to consider:

1. Physical Self-Care: Engage in activities that promote physical health, such as regular exercise, a balanced diet, and adequate sleep. Take time for relaxation and rest to support your body's needs.

2. Emotional Self-Care: Practice activities that nurture your emotional well-being, such as journaling, expressing your feelings, and engaging in creative outlets. Allow yourself to experience and process emotions without judgment.

3. Mental Self-Care: Stimulate your mind with activities that promote intellectual growth, such as reading, learning new skills, and solving puzzles. Take breaks from mental tasks to avoid cognitive overload.

4. Spiritual Self-Care: Engage in practices that nurture your spiritual well-being, such as meditation, prayer, or spending time in nature. Reflect on your values and beliefs to find meaning and purpose.

Setting Boundaries

SETTING BOUNDARIES is crucial for protecting your well-being and preventing burnout. Here are some strategies for setting healthy boundaries:

1. Know Your Limits: Understand your limits and recognize when you need to set boundaries. Pay attention to your energy levels and feelings of overwhelm.

2. Communicate Clearly: Clearly communicate your boundaries to others. Use assertive language and be specific about your needs and expectations.

3. Practice Saying No: Learn to say no when necessary to protect your time and energy. Saying no to additional commitments or tasks can prevent overloading yourself.

4. Prioritize Self-Care: Make self-care a priority and schedule time for activities that support your well-being. Protect this time from other demands and responsibilities.

5. Seek Support: Reach out for support from trusted friends, family members, or professionals when you need help setting and maintaining boundaries.

Real-Life Applications and Success Stories

TO ILLUSTRATE THE EFFECTIVENESS of lifestyle changes for anxiety management, here are real-life applications and success stories of individuals who have made intentional choices to build healthier routines and reduce their anxiety.

Case Study 1: Transforming Anxiety with Diet and Exercise

BACKGROUND: LISA IS a 35-year-old graphic designer who has struggled with anxiety for years. Her anxiety often manifests as physical tension and digestive issues. Lisa's diet consisted of processed foods, high sugar intake, and frequent consumption of caffeine. She also led a sedentary lifestyle with little physical activity.

Lifestyle Changes: With the help of a nutritionist and a fitness coach, Lisa made significant changes to her diet and exercise routine. She incorporated nutrient-rich foods into her diet, such as leafy greens, fatty fish, nuts, seeds, and whole grains. She reduced her sugar and caffeine intake and focused on eating whole, unprocessed foods. Lisa also began a regular exercise routine that included aerobic activities, strength training, and yoga.

Results: After several months of consistent diet and exercise changes, Lisa noticed a significant reduction in her anxiety levels. Her physical tension and digestive issues improved, and she felt more energized and focused. By building a healthier routine, Lisa was able to manage her anxiety more effectively and enhance her overall well-being.

Case Study 2: Improving Sleep and Work-Life Balance

BACKGROUND: MICHAEL is a 40-year-old lawyer who has been experiencing chronic stress and anxiety due to his demanding job. His work often required long hours, late nights, and frequent travel. Michael's sleep quality was poor, and he struggled to maintain a healthy work-life balance.

Lifestyle Changes: Michael decided to prioritize his sleep and work-life balance to reduce his anxiety. He established a consistent sleep routine by going to bed and waking up at the same time every day. He created a relaxing bedtime routine that included reading, taking a warm bath, and practicing relaxation techniques. Michael also set clear boundaries between work and personal time, avoiding work-related tasks during his personal time. He scheduled regular breaks throughout his workday and delegated tasks to colleagues when possible.

Results: After implementing these changes, Michael's sleep quality improved significantly, and he felt more rested and alert during the day. He experienced a reduction in stress and anxiety and found it easier to manage his workload. By prioritizing sleep and work-life balance, Michael was able to reduce his anxiety and improve his overall quality of life.

Case Study 3: Enhancing Emotional Well-Being with Self-Care and Boundaries

BACKGROUND: EMILY IS a 28-year-old teacher who has been experiencing burnout and anxiety due to her demanding job and lack of self-care. She often felt overwhelmed and struggled to set boundaries with her students, colleagues, and family members.

Lifestyle Changes: Emily decided to prioritize self-care and set healthy boundaries to manage her anxiety. She incorporated physical, emotional, mental, and spiritual self-care practices into her routine. Emily started a regular exercise routine, practiced mindfulness meditation, and engaged in creative activities such as painting and journaling. She also set clear boundaries with her students, colleagues, and family members, communicating her needs and saying no to additional commitments when necessary.

Results: After several months of consistent self-care and boundary-setting, Emily noticed a significant improvement in her emotional well-being. She felt more balanced, energized, and in control of her life. Her anxiety levels decreased, and she found it easier to manage stress. By prioritizing self-care and setting boundaries, Emily was able to reduce her anxiety and enhance her overall well-being.

Conclusion

Building a healthier routine through intentional lifestyle changes can play a crucial role in managing anxiety and enhancing overall well-being. By making informed choices about diet, exercise, sleep, self-care, and boundaries, individuals can create a balanced lifestyle that supports their mental health.

A balanced diet rich in essential nutrients, regular physical activity, and adequate sleep are fundamental components of a healthy routine. Incorporating self-care practices and setting boundaries are essential for protecting well-being and preventing burnout.

Real-life applications and success stories, such as those of Lisa, Michael, and Emily, demonstrate the effectiveness of lifestyle changes for anxiety management. Their experiences highlight the positive impact of building a healthier routine and the potential for change and recovery.

Remember, managing anxiety is a journey that requires patience, persistence, and support. With the right knowledge, resources, and techniques, you can take control of your anxiety and work toward a future free from excessive fear and stress.

Chapter 9: Medication and Alternative Therapies

Exploring Treatment Options

Managing anxiety and phobias often involves a combination of different treatment modalities. While some individuals may benefit from cognitive-behavioral therapy (CBT) and lifestyle changes alone, others may require medication or alternative therapies to achieve optimal results. This chapter provides an overview of medications for anxiety and phobias, discusses the pros and cons of pharmacological treatments, and explores various alternative therapies, including acupuncture, herbal remedies, and more.

Overview of Medications for Anxiety and Phobias

MEDICATIONS CAN BE an effective part of a comprehensive treatment plan for anxiety and phobias. They can help manage symptoms, reduce the intensity of anxiety, and improve overall functioning. The primary classes of medications used to treat anxiety and phobias include selective serotonin reuptake inhibitors (SSRIs), serotonin-norepinephrine reuptake inhibitors (SNRIs), benzodiazepines, and beta-blockers.

Selective Serotonin Reuptake Inhibitors (SSRIs)

SSRIS ARE A CLASS OF antidepressants commonly prescribed to treat anxiety disorders and phobias. They work by increasing the levels of serotonin, a neurotransmitter that plays a key role in mood regulation, in the brain. Common SSRIs include:

1. Fluoxetine (Prozac): Often prescribed for generalized anxiety disorder (GAD), social anxiety disorder (SAD), and panic disorder.

2. Sertraline (Zoloft): Used to treat GAD, SAD, panic disorder, and post-traumatic stress disorder (PTSD).

3. Escitalopram (Lexapro): Effective for GAD and SAD.

4. Paroxetine (Paxil): Prescribed for GAD, SAD, panic disorder, and PTSD.

5. Citalopram (Celexa): Used for GAD and other anxiety disorders.

Serotonin-Norepinephrine Reuptake Inhibitors (SNRIs)

SNRIS ARE ANOTHER CLASS of antidepressants that work by increasing the levels of both serotonin and norepinephrine in the brain. Common SNRIs include:

1. Venlafaxine (Effexor): Effective for GAD, SAD, and panic disorder.

2. Duloxetine (Cymbalta): Used to treat GAD and can also help with chronic pain conditions that may co-occur with anxiety.

Benzodiazepines

Benzodiazepines are fast-acting medications that provide short-term relief for acute anxiety symptoms. They work by enhancing the effects of gamma-aminobutyric acid (GABA), a neurotransmitter that inhibits nervous system activity. Common benzodiazepines include:

1. Diazepam (Valium): Used for acute anxiety episodes and panic attacks.

2. Alprazolam (Xanax): Prescribed for panic disorder and acute anxiety.

3. Lorazepam (Ativan): Effective for anxiety, panic attacks, and insomnia related to anxiety.

4. Clonazepam (Klonopin): Used for panic disorder and certain types of phobias.

Beta-Blockers

BETA-BLOCKERS ARE MEDICATIONS that reduce the physical symptoms of anxiety, such as rapid heart rate and trembling, by blocking the effects of adrenaline. They are commonly used for situational anxiety, such as performance anxiety or specific phobias. Common beta-blockers include:

1. Propranolol (Inderal): Often prescribed for performance anxiety and situational phobias.

2. Atenolol (Tenormin): Used for similar purposes as propranolol.

Pros and Cons of Pharmacological Treatments

WHILE MEDICATIONS CAN be highly effective in managing anxiety and phobias, they also come with potential benefits and drawbacks. Understanding the pros and cons of pharmacological treatments can help individuals make informed decisions about their treatment options.

Pros of Pharmacological Treatments

1. RAPID SYMPTOM RELIEF: Medications, especially benzodiazepines, can provide rapid relief from acute anxiety symptoms, making them useful for managing severe episodes or panic attacks.

2. Improvement in Quality of Life: By reducing the intensity and frequency of anxiety symptoms, medications can significantly improve an individual's quality of life and ability to function in daily activities.

3. Adjunct to Therapy: Medications can be used in conjunction with psychotherapy, such as CBT, to enhance treatment outcomes. They can help individuals manage symptoms more effectively, allowing them to engage more fully in therapy.

4. Variety of Options: There are multiple classes of medications available, allowing for personalized treatment plans based on an individual's specific needs and response to medication.

Cons of Pharmacological Treatments

1. SIDE EFFECTS: MANY medications come with potential side effects, which can range from mild to severe. Common side effects of SSRIs and SNRIs include nausea, headaches, insomnia, sexual dysfunction, and weight gain. Benzodiazepines can cause drowsiness, dizziness, and impaired coordination.

2. Risk of Dependence and Withdrawal: Benzodiazepines carry a risk of dependence and withdrawal symptoms, particularly with long-term use. Abrupt discontinuation of benzodiazepines can lead to withdrawal symptoms such as increased anxiety, insomnia, and agitation.

3. Delayed Onset of Action: While benzodiazepines provide rapid relief, SSRIs and SNRIs may take several weeks to achieve their full therapeutic effect. This delayed onset can be challenging for individuals seeking immediate relief.

4. Medication Interactions: Certain medications can interact with other drugs, leading to potentially harmful effects. It is important to disclose all medications and supplements to the prescribing healthcare provider.

5. Individual Variability: Response to medication can vary widely among individuals. What works for one person may not work for another, and finding the right medication and dosage can involve a trial-and-error process.

Alternative Therapies: Acupuncture, Herbal Remedies, and More

IN ADDITION TO PHARMACOLOGICAL treatments, various alternative therapies can be effective in managing anxiety and phobias. These therapies can be used alone or in combination with conventional treatments to enhance overall well-being.

Acupuncture

ACUPUNCTURE IS A TRADITIONAL Chinese medicine practice that involves inserting thin needles into specific points on the body to balance the flow of energy (Qi). It is believed to promote healing and relieve symptoms of various conditions, including anxiety.

How Acupuncture Works:

- Acupuncture is thought to stimulate the body's natural painkillers, such as endorphins, and influence the autonomic nervous system to promote relaxation and reduce stress.

- It may also regulate the hypothalamic-pituitary-adrenal (HPA) axis, which plays a key role in the body's stress response.

Benefits of Acupuncture for Anxiety:

- Acupuncture can provide immediate relief from anxiety symptoms and promote a sense of calm and well-being.

- It is a non-invasive and drug-free treatment option with minimal side effects.

- Regular acupuncture sessions can improve overall mental and physical health.

Considerations:

- Acupuncture should be performed by a licensed and experienced practitioner to ensure safety and effectiveness.

- It may not be suitable for individuals with certain medical conditions or those who have a fear of needles.

Herbal Remedies

HERBAL REMEDIES HAVE been used for centuries to treat various health conditions, including anxiety. Some herbs have calming and anxiolytic properties that can help reduce anxiety symptoms.

Common Herbal Remedies for Anxiety:

1. Valerian Root: Valerian root is known for its sedative and calming effects. It is often used to promote relaxation and improve sleep quality.

2. Passionflower: Passionflower is believed to have anxiolytic properties and can help reduce symptoms of anxiety and insomnia.

3. Chamomile: Chamomile is commonly used as a mild sedative and relaxant. Chamomile tea is a popular remedy for promoting relaxation and reducing anxiety.

4. Lavender: Lavender has calming and soothing properties. It can be used in various forms, such as essential oil, tea, or supplements, to reduce anxiety.

5. Ashwagandha: Ashwagandha is an adaptogenic herb that helps the body adapt to stress and reduce anxiety. It is often used in Ayurvedic medicine.

6. Lemon Balm: Lemon balm is known for its calming effects and can help reduce symptoms of anxiety and improve mood.

Benefits of Herbal Remedies:

- Herbal remedies are natural and generally have fewer side effects compared to conventional medications.

- They can be used as complementary treatments alongside other therapies.

- Herbal remedies are accessible and can be incorporated into daily routines, such as drinking herbal teas.

Considerations:

- Herbal remedies can interact with other medications, so it is important to consult with a healthcare provider before using them.

- The quality and potency of herbal products can vary, so it is important to choose reputable brands and sources.

- Some individuals may be allergic to certain herbs, so it is important to start with small doses and monitor for any adverse reactions.

Mind-Body Practices

MIND-BODY PRACTICES, such as yoga, tai chi, and qigong, combine physical movement, breath control, and meditation to promote relaxation and reduce anxiety.

Yoga: Yoga involves physical postures, breathing exercises, and meditation to promote physical and mental well-being. Regular yoga practice can reduce anxiety, improve mood, and enhance overall health.

Tai Chi: Tai chi is a Chinese martial art that involves slow, deliberate movements and deep breathing. It is often described as "meditation in motion" and can reduce stress and anxiety.

Qigong: Qigong is a practice that involves coordinated movements, breath control, and meditation to promote the flow of energy (Qi) in the body. It can enhance relaxation and reduce anxiety.

Benefits of Mind-Body Practices:

- Mind-body practices promote relaxation, reduce stress, and improve mental clarity.

- They enhance physical health by improving flexibility, strength, and balance.

- These practices can be easily incorporated into daily routines and adapted to individual preferences.

Considerations:

- It is important to learn proper techniques from qualified instructors to ensure safety and effectiveness.

- Consistency and regular practice are key to achieving the full benefits of mind-body practices.

Aromatherapy

Aromatherapy involves the use of essential oils to promote relaxation and reduce anxiety. Essential oils can be inhaled, applied to the skin, or used in diffusers to create a calming environment.

Common Essential Oils for Anxiety:

1. Lavender: Lavender essential oil is known for its calming and soothing effects. It can be used to promote relaxation and improve sleep quality.

2. Bergamot: Bergamot essential oil has uplifting and calming properties. It can help reduce anxiety and improve mood.

3. Frankincense: Frankincense essential oil is believed to have grounding and calming effects. It can be used to reduce stress and promote a sense of peace.

4. Chamomile: Chamomile essential oil has calming and relaxing properties. It can help reduce anxiety and promote relaxation.

5. Ylang-Ylang: Ylang-ylang essential oil is known for its calming and sedative effects. It can help reduce anxiety and improve mood.

Benefits of Aromatherapy:

- Aromatherapy is a non-invasive and natural treatment option with minimal side effects.

- It can create a calming and relaxing environment, enhancing overall well-being.

- Essential oils can be used in various ways, such as inhalation, massage, or bath, to suit individual preferences.

Considerations:

- Essential oils should be used with caution and diluted properly to avoid skin irritation or allergic reactions.

- It is important to choose high-quality essential oils from reputable sources.

- Some individuals may be sensitive to certain scents, so it is important to start with small amounts and monitor for any adverse reactions.

Combining Conventional and Alternative Therapies

COMBINING CONVENTIONAL treatments, such as medication and psychotherapy, with alternative therapies can provide a comprehensive and holistic approach to managing anxiety and phobias. Here are some strategies for integrating different treatment modalities:

1. Consult with Healthcare Providers: Before starting any new treatment, it is important to consult with healthcare providers, including primary care physicians, psychiatrists, and alternative therapy practitioners. They can provide guidance, monitor progress, and ensure the safety and effectiveness of combined treatments.

2. Create a Personalized Treatment Plan: Work with healthcare providers to create a personalized treatment plan that addresses individual needs and preferences. This plan may include a combination of medication, psychotherapy, lifestyle changes, and alternative therapies.

3. Monitor Progress and Adjust as Needed: Regularly monitor progress and assess the effectiveness of different treatments. Adjust the treatment plan as needed based on individual response and feedback from healthcare providers.

4. Practice Self-Care: Incorporate self-care practices into the treatment plan to support overall well-being. This may include regular exercise, healthy eating, adequate sleep, relaxation techniques, and social support.

5. Stay Informed: Stay informed about the latest research and developments in both conventional and alternative treatments for anxiety and phobias. Being informed can help individuals make educated decisions about their treatment options.

Real-Life Applications and Success Stories

TO ILLUSTRATE THE EFFECTIVENESS of combining conventional and alternative therapies, here are real-life applications and success stories of individuals who have used an integrative approach to manage anxiety and phobias.

Case Study 1: Integrating Medication and Acupuncture

BACKGROUND: JOHN IS a 45-year-old engineer who has been experiencing generalized anxiety disorder (GAD) for several years. His symptoms include chronic worry, muscle tension, and insomnia. John was prescribed an SSRI (sertraline) by his psychiatrist, which provided some relief but did not fully alleviate his symptoms.

Alternative Therapy: John decided to try acupuncture as a complementary treatment to enhance his medication regimen. He began regular acupuncture sessions with a licensed practitioner who specialized in anxiety management.

Results: After several weeks of combining medication with acupuncture, John noticed a significant reduction in his anxiety symptoms. His muscle tension decreased, and he experienced improved sleep quality. The combination of SSRI and acupuncture provided a more comprehensive approach to managing his GAD.

Case Study 2: Combining Herbal Remedies and Cognitive-Behavioral Therapy (CBT)

BACKGROUND: EMILY IS a 30-year-old teacher who has been struggling with social anxiety disorder (SAD). Her symptoms included intense fear of social interactions, avoidance of social situations, and difficulty speaking in public. Emily began CBT with a therapist to address her negative thought patterns and avoidance behaviors.

Alternative Therapy: In addition to CBT, Emily decided to try herbal remedies to support her treatment. She started taking a combination of passionflower and lemon balm supplements, known for their calming and anxiolytic properties.

Results: After several months of combining CBT with herbal remedies, Emily experienced significant improvements in her social anxiety. She became more comfortable in social situations, engaged more actively in conversations, and successfully gave presentations at work. The combination of CBT and herbal remedies provided a holistic approach to managing her SAD.

Case Study 3: Utilizing Yoga and Aromatherapy for Panic Disorder

BACKGROUND: SARAH IS a 35-year-old nurse who has been experiencing panic disorder. Her symptoms included recurrent panic attacks, rapid heart rate, shortness of breath, and fear of losing control. Sarah was prescribed a benzodiazepine (clonazepam) for acute panic attacks, but she wanted to explore additional therapies to manage her symptoms.

Alternative Therapy: Sarah decided to incorporate yoga and aromatherapy into her treatment plan. She began attending regular yoga classes and used essential oils, such as lavender and bergamot, in a diffuser and for topical application.

Results: After several months of practicing yoga and using aromatherapy, Sarah noticed a significant reduction in the frequency and intensity of her panic attacks. She felt more grounded, calm, and in control of her anxiety. The combination of medication, yoga, and aromatherapy provided a comprehensive approach to managing her panic disorder.

Conclusion

Managing anxiety and phobias often requires a multifaceted approach that includes both conventional and alternative therapies. Medications, such as SSRIs, SNRIs, benzodiazepines, and beta-blockers, can provide effective relief from anxiety symptoms, while alternative therapies, such as acupuncture, herbal remedies, mind-body practices, and aromatherapy, offer additional support.

Understanding the pros and cons of pharmacological treatments, as well as the benefits and considerations of alternative therapies, can help individuals make informed decisions about their treatment options. Combining conventional and alternative therapies can provide a comprehensive and holistic approach to managing anxiety and phobias.

Real-life applications and success stories, such as those of John, Emily, and Sarah, demonstrate the potential for change and recovery with an integrative approach to treatment. Their experiences highlight the effectiveness of combining different treatment modalities to achieve optimal results.

Remember, managing anxiety and phobias is a journey that requires patience, persistence, and support. With the right knowledge, resources, and treatment plan, you can take control of your anxiety and work toward a future free from excessive fear and stress.

Chapter 10: Support Systems and Social Connections

Building Your Support Network

Support systems and social connections play a crucial role in the recovery and management of anxiety and phobias. They provide emotional support, practical assistance, and a sense of belonging, all of which are vital for maintaining mental health and well-being. This chapter explores the role of family and friends in recovery, the benefits of joining support groups and online communities, and the importance of professional support from therapists and counselors.

The Role of Family and Friends in Recovery

FAMILY AND FRIENDS are often the first line of support for individuals dealing with anxiety and phobias. Their understanding, encouragement, and assistance can make a significant difference in the recovery process.

Emotional Support

EMOTIONAL SUPPORT FROM family and friends involves providing a safe and understanding environment where individuals feel comfortable expressing their thoughts and feelings. This type of support can help alleviate feelings of isolation, reduce stress, and improve overall mental health.

Key Elements of Emotional Support:

1. Active Listening: Family and friends can provide emotional support by actively listening to the individual's concerns without judgment or interruption. This involves giving full attention, validating their feelings, and offering empathy.

2. Empathy and Understanding: Demonstrating empathy involves putting oneself in the other person's shoes and understanding their emotions and experiences. Offering understanding and reassurance can help individuals feel heard and supported.

3. Encouragement and Positive Reinforcement: Encouraging words and positive reinforcement can boost self-esteem and motivate individuals to continue their recovery efforts. Celebrating small achievements and progress can foster a sense of accomplishment.

Practical Assistance

PRACTICAL ASSISTANCE involves helping individuals manage their daily responsibilities and challenges. This type of support can alleviate stress and create a more manageable environment for recovery.

Examples of Practical Assistance:

1. Daily Tasks: Family and friends can help with daily tasks such as household chores, grocery shopping, or childcare. This support can reduce the burden on the individual and allow them to focus on their recovery.

2. Accompanying to Appointments: Offering to accompany individuals to therapy or medical appointments can provide reassurance and support. This presence can reduce anxiety and help individuals feel more comfortable.

3. Providing Resources: Family and friends can help gather information about treatment options, support groups, and other resources. Sharing relevant articles, books, or websites can empower individuals with knowledge and support their recovery journey.

Creating a Supportive Environment

CREATING A SUPPORTIVE environment involves making changes at home and within social circles to promote recovery and well-being. A positive and nurturing environment can significantly impact an individual's mental health.

Strategies for Creating a Supportive Environment:

1. Open Communication: Encourage open and honest communication within the family or social circle. Create a space where individuals feel comfortable discussing their feelings and experiences without fear of judgment.

2. Reducing Stressors: Identify and reduce potential stressors within the environment. This may involve establishing a calm and organized home, setting boundaries, and managing conflicts constructively.

3. Promoting Healthy Habits: Encourage and model healthy habits such as regular exercise, balanced nutrition, adequate sleep, and relaxation techniques. Supporting these habits can contribute to overall well-being and reduce anxiety.

Joining Support Groups and Online Communities

SUPPORT GROUPS AND online communities provide opportunities for individuals to connect with others who share similar experiences. These groups offer a sense of belonging, mutual support, and valuable insights into managing anxiety and phobias.

Benefits of Support Groups

SUPPORT GROUPS CONSIST of individuals who come together to share their experiences, challenges, and successes in managing anxiety and phobias. These groups can be led by a professional facilitator or peer-led.

Key Benefits of Support Groups:

1. Shared Experiences: Hearing from others who have faced similar challenges can provide comfort and validation. Sharing experiences can help individuals feel less alone and more understood.

2. Emotional Support: Support groups offer a safe space to express emotions and receive empathy and encouragement from others. This emotional support can reduce feelings of isolation and promote healing.

3. Practical Advice: Members of support groups often share practical advice and coping strategies that have worked for them. This collective wisdom can provide new perspectives and solutions for managing anxiety and phobias.

4. Accountability and Motivation: Being part of a group can provide accountability and motivation to stay committed to recovery goals. Regular meetings and check-ins can encourage progress and consistency.

Types of Support Groups

THERE ARE VARIOUS TYPES of support groups, each catering to different needs and preferences. Finding the right group can enhance the support and benefits received.

Types of Support Groups:

1. In-Person Support Groups: These groups meet face-to-face in a physical location, such as a community center, hospital, or therapist's office. In-person interactions can foster deeper connections and a sense of community.

2. Online Support Groups: Online groups provide a convenient and accessible option for individuals who may not have local support groups available. These groups meet virtually through video calls, forums, or social media platforms.

3. Condition-Specific Groups: Some support groups focus on specific types of anxiety or phobias, such as social anxiety, panic disorder, or agoraphobia. These groups can provide specialized support and resources tailored to specific conditions.

4. Peer-Led Groups: Peer-led groups are facilitated by individuals who have personal experience with anxiety and phobias. These facilitators offer unique insights and empathy, creating a relatable and supportive environment.

Finding and Joining Support Groups

FINDING THE RIGHT SUPPORT group involves exploring available options and determining which group aligns with individual needs and preferences.

Steps to Finding and Joining Support Groups:

1. Research Available Groups: Start by researching available support groups in your area or online. Look for groups that focus on anxiety and phobias and consider factors such as meeting times, locations, and group size.

2. Attend Initial Meetings: Attend a few initial meetings to get a sense of the group dynamics and whether it feels like a good fit. Observe how the group operates, the level of support provided, and the overall atmosphere.

3. Seek Recommendations: Ask healthcare providers, therapists, or other individuals in your support network for recommendations. They may have knowledge of reputable support groups that align with your needs.

4. Evaluate Fit: After attending a few meetings, evaluate whether the group meets your needs and provides the support you seek. Consider factors such as the group's focus, the facilitator's approach, and the level of connection with other members.

Online Communities

ONLINE COMMUNITIES offer additional opportunities for connection and support. These communities can be accessed from anywhere and provide a platform for sharing experiences, seeking advice, and building connections.

Benefits of Online Communities:

1. Accessibility: Online communities are accessible to individuals regardless of location. This makes them a valuable resource for those who may not have local support groups available.

2. Anonymity: Online platforms often allow for anonymity, which can encourage individuals to share openly and honestly without fear of judgment.

3. 24/7 Availability: Online communities are available around the clock, providing support whenever it is needed. This can be especially helpful during times of heightened anxiety or distress.

4. Diverse Perspectives: Online communities bring together individuals from various backgrounds and experiences, offering a diverse range of perspectives and insights.

Popular Online Platforms for Support:

1. Social Media Groups: Platforms such as Facebook and Reddit have numerous groups dedicated to anxiety and phobias. These groups provide a space for discussion, sharing resources, and offering support.

2. Mental Health Forums: Websites such as Psych Central and Anxiety and Depression Association of America (ADAA) offer forums where individuals can post questions, share experiences, and connect with others.

3. Online Therapy Platforms: Some online therapy platforms, such as BetterHelp and Talkspace, offer group therapy sessions and support groups as part of their services.

Professional Support: Therapists and Counselors

PROFESSIONAL SUPPORT from therapists and counselors is a critical component of a comprehensive treatment plan for anxiety and phobias. These professionals provide evidence-based therapies, guidance, and support to help individuals manage their symptoms and achieve their recovery goals.

Types of Therapists and Counselors

THERE ARE VARIOUS TYPES of mental health professionals, each with their own areas of expertise and approaches to treatment. Understanding the different types can help individuals choose the right professional for their needs.

Types of Therapists and Counselors:

1. Clinical Psychologists: Clinical psychologists hold a doctoral degree (Ph.D. or Psy.D.) and specialize in diagnosing and treating mental health disorders. They use evidence-based therapies such as cognitive-behavioral therapy (CBT), exposure therapy, and dialectical behavior therapy (DBT).

2. Licensed Professional Counselors (LPCs): LPCs hold a master's degree in counseling and are trained to provide individual, group, and family therapy. They use various therapeutic approaches to address anxiety and phobias.

3. Psychiatrists: Psychiatrists are medical doctors (M.D. or D.O.) who specialize in diagnosing and treating mental health disorders. They can prescribe medication and provide therapy. Psychiatrists often work in conjunction with therapists and counselors to provide comprehensive care.

4. Licensed Clinical Social Workers (LCSWs): LCSWs hold a master's degree in social work and are trained to provide therapy and support for mental health issues. They often focus on the social and environmental factors that contribute to anxiety and phobias.

5. Marriage and Family Therapists (MFTs): MFTs hold a master's degree in marriage and family therapy and specialize in treating individuals, couples, and families. They address relational dynamics and how they impact mental health.

Evidence-Based Therapies

THERAPISTS AND COUNSELORS use evidence-based therapies to treat anxiety and phobias. These therapies are supported by research and have been proven effective in reducing symptoms and improving quality of life.

Common Evidence-Based Therapies:

1. Cognitive-Behavioral Therapy (CBT): CBT is a widely used therapy that focuses on identifying and changing negative thought patterns and behaviors. It helps individuals develop healthier ways of thinking and coping with anxiety.

2. Exposure Therapy: Exposure therapy involves gradually and systematically exposing individuals to feared situations or objects to reduce avoidance and anxiety. This therapy is particularly effective for phobias and PTSD.

3. Dialectical Behavior Therapy (DBT): DBT is a form of CBT that focuses on building skills in mindfulness, emotional regulation, distress tolerance, and interpersonal effectiveness. It is effective for individuals with anxiety and emotional dysregulation.

4. Acceptance and Commitment Therapy (ACT): ACT helps individuals accept their thoughts and feelings rather than trying to change them. It emphasizes living in accordance with one's values and committing to actions that improve quality of life.

5. Eye Movement Desensitization and Reprocessing (EMDR): EMDR is used to treat trauma and PTSD by helping individuals process traumatic memories through guided eye movements. It can also be effective for certain anxiety disorders.

Finding and Choosing a Therapist or Counselor

FINDING THE RIGHT THERAPIST or counselor involves researching options, evaluating credentials, and determining the best fit for individual needs and preferences.

Steps to Finding and Choosing a Therapist or Counselor:

1. Research Options: Start by researching available therapists and counselors in your area or online. Look for professionals who specialize in anxiety and phobias and offer evidence-based therapies.

2. Check Credentials: Verify the credentials and licensing of potential therapists and counselors. Ensure they are licensed to practice in your state and have the appropriate training and experience.

3. Read Reviews and Testimonials: Reading reviews and testimonials from other clients can provide insights into the therapist's approach and effectiveness. Look for positive feedback and evidence of successful outcomes.

4. Schedule Consultations: Schedule initial consultations with a few potential therapists to discuss your needs and treatment goals. This allows you to evaluate their approach, communication style, and compatibility.

5. Evaluate Fit: After the consultations, evaluate which therapist feels like the best fit for you. Consider factors such as their approach, personality, and your comfort level during the session.

The Role of Therapy in Recovery

THERAPY PLAYS A VITAL role in the recovery process by providing structured support, guidance, and tools for managing anxiety and phobias. It helps individuals develop coping strategies, build resilience, and work toward their recovery goals.

Key Roles of Therapy in Recovery:

1. Assessment and Diagnosis: Therapists conduct thorough assessments to diagnose anxiety and phobias accurately. Understanding the specific condition allows for tailored treatment plans.

2. Treatment Planning: Therapists collaborate with individuals to develop personalized treatment plans that address their unique needs and goals. This plan may include various therapeutic approaches and interventions.

3. Skill Building: Therapy focuses on building skills to manage anxiety, such as relaxation techniques, cognitive restructuring, and exposure exercises. These skills empower individuals to cope with anxiety effectively.

4. Emotional Processing: Therapy provides a safe space for individuals to process and understand their emotions. This emotional processing can lead to greater self-awareness and emotional regulation.

5. Support and Accountability: Therapists offer ongoing support and accountability throughout the recovery journey. Regular sessions provide opportunities to discuss progress, address challenges, and adjust the treatment plan as needed.

Real-Life Applications and Success Stories

TO ILLUSTRATE THE EFFECTIVENESS of building a support network, here are real-life applications and success stories of individuals who have benefited from the support of family and friends, support groups, and professional therapists.

Case Study 1: Overcoming Social Anxiety with Family Support and Therapy

BACKGROUND: MARK IS a 28-year-old software developer who has been struggling with social anxiety disorder (SAD). His symptoms included intense fear of social interactions, avoidance of social situations, and difficulty speaking in public.

Support System: Mark's family played a crucial role in his recovery by providing emotional support, encouragement, and practical assistance. They actively listened to his concerns, validated his feelings, and encouraged him to seek professional help.

Therapy: Mark began cognitive-behavioral therapy (CBT) with a licensed therapist who specialized in anxiety disorders. Through CBT, he learned to identify and challenge negative thought patterns and gradually expose himself to social situations.

Results: With the support of his family and the guidance of his therapist, Mark made significant progress in managing his social anxiety. He became more comfortable in social interactions, engaged more actively in conversations, and successfully gave presentations at work. The combination of family support and professional therapy provided a comprehensive approach to his recovery.

Case Study 2: Finding Strength in a Support Group

BACKGROUND: EMILY IS a 35-year-old teacher who has been experiencing generalized anxiety disorder (GAD) for several years. Her symptoms included chronic worry, muscle tension, and difficulty concentrating.

Support Group: Emily joined a local support group for individuals with anxiety disorders. The group provided a safe space for sharing experiences, receiving empathy, and learning coping strategies from others who faced similar challenges.

Therapy: In addition to the support group, Emily attended individual therapy sessions with a licensed counselor. Her therapist helped her develop personalized coping strategies and provided ongoing support and accountability.

Results: The support group offered Emily a sense of belonging and validation, while therapy provided structured guidance and skill-building. Together, these resources helped Emily reduce her anxiety, improve her ability to manage stress, and enhance her overall well-being.

Case Study 3: Utilizing Online Communities and Professional Support

BACKGROUND: SARAH IS a 30-year-old nurse who has been experiencing panic disorder. Her symptoms included recurrent panic attacks, rapid heart rate, and fear of losing control.

Online Community: Sarah joined an online community dedicated to individuals with panic disorder. The community provided 24/7 support, allowing her to connect with others, share experiences, and seek advice at any time.

Therapy: Sarah also began therapy with a licensed clinical psychologist who specialized in panic disorder. Through cognitive-behavioral therapy (CBT) and exposure therapy, Sarah learned to manage her panic attacks and reduce avoidance behaviors.

Results: The online community offered Sarah immediate and ongoing support, while therapy provided evidence-based interventions and personalized guidance. This combination helped Sarah reduce the frequency and intensity of her panic attacks, gain confidence in her ability to manage her anxiety, and improve her quality of life.

Conclusion

Building a support network is essential for managing anxiety and phobias and achieving recovery. Family and friends provide emotional support, practical assistance, and a supportive environment that fosters healing and well-being. Joining support groups and online communities offers additional opportunities for connection, shared experiences, and mutual support.

Professional support from therapists and counselors provides evidence-based therapies, guidance, and tools for managing anxiety and phobias. Combining the support of family, friends, support groups, and professional therapists creates a comprehensive and holistic approach to recovery.

Real-life applications and success stories, such as those of Mark, Emily, and Sarah, demonstrate the effectiveness of building a support network. Their experiences highlight the positive impact of support systems and social connections on mental health and well-being.

Remember, managing anxiety and phobias is a journey that requires patience, persistence, and support. With the right knowledge, resources, and a strong support network, you can take control of your anxiety and work toward a future free from excessive fear and stress.

Chapter 11: Coping Strategies for Daily Life

Practical Tips for Managing Anxiety

Anxiety can be overwhelming, but with the right strategies and tools, it is possible to manage it effectively in daily life. This chapter provides practical tips for handling anxiety in various situations, offers guidance on creating an anxiety management plan, and explores how technology and apps can support anxiety management.

Techniques for Handling Anxiety in Various Situations

ANXIETY CAN ARISE IN different contexts, such as work, social settings, or everyday activities. Developing specific coping strategies for each situation can help manage anxiety and improve overall well-being.

Work-Related Anxiety

WORK-RELATED ANXIETY can stem from various sources, including workload, deadlines, interactions with colleagues, and job performance. Here are some techniques for managing anxiety in the workplace:

1. Prioritize and Organize Tasks:

- Create a To-Do List: Write down all tasks that need to be completed and prioritize them based on urgency and importance.

- Break Tasks into Smaller Steps: Breaking tasks into smaller, manageable steps can make them feel less overwhelming and more achievable.

- Use a Planner or Digital Tool: Utilize a planner or digital tool to keep track of deadlines and appointments. This can help you stay organized and reduce anxiety about forgetting important tasks.

2. Practice Time Management:

- Set Realistic Goals: Set achievable goals for each day and avoid overcommitting to tasks. This can help prevent feeling overwhelmed.

- Take Regular Breaks: Schedule short breaks throughout the day to rest and recharge. Taking breaks can improve focus and productivity.

- Use the Pomodoro Technique: Work for 25 minutes, then take a 5-minute break. After four cycles, take a longer break. This technique can help maintain focus and reduce burnout.

3. Develop Effective Communication Skills:

- Assertive Communication: Practice assertive communication by expressing your needs and boundaries clearly and respectfully. This can help reduce stress and improve interactions with colleagues.

- Active Listening: Practice active listening by giving your full attention to the speaker, asking clarifying questions, and providing feedback. Effective communication can prevent misunderstandings and reduce anxiety.

- Seek Support: If you are feeling overwhelmed, talk to your supervisor or a trusted colleague. Asking for support or delegating tasks can help manage workload and reduce stress.

4. Create a Calming Workspace:

- Organize Your Workspace: Keep your workspace tidy and organized to reduce distractions and create a calming environment.

- Personalize Your Space: Add personal touches, such as photos, plants, or calming colors, to make your workspace more comfortable and relaxing.

- Practice Deep Breathing: Take a few moments to practice deep breathing exercises during stressful moments. This can help calm your mind and body.

Social Anxiety

SOCIAL ANXIETY INVOLVES intense fear of social situations and interactions. It can make everyday activities, such as attending events or speaking in public, challenging. Here are some techniques for managing social anxiety:

1. Gradual Exposure:

- Start Small: Begin by exposing yourself to less intimidating social situations and gradually work your way up to more challenging ones. For example, start by attending small gatherings before moving on to larger events.

- Use a Support Person: Bring a trusted friend or family member to social events for support and encouragement. Having someone familiar can help reduce anxiety.

- Set Achievable Goals: Set small, achievable goals for each social interaction. For example, aim to start a conversation with one person at a party.

2. Challenge Negative Thoughts:

- Identify Negative Thoughts: Pay attention to negative thoughts that arise in social situations, such as "Everyone is judging me" or "I'll embarrass myself."

- Challenge and Reframe: Challenge these thoughts by considering evidence against them and reframing them in a more positive light. For example, remind yourself that most people are focused on themselves and not judging you.

3. Practice Social Skills:

- Role-Playing: Practice social interactions through role-playing with a trusted friend or therapist. This can help build confidence and reduce anxiety in real-life situations.

- Active Listening: Focus on listening to others and showing interest in what they are saying. Active listening can improve social interactions and reduce self-consciousness.

- Mindfulness: Practice mindfulness to stay present in social situations. Focus on the current moment rather than worrying about what others think.

4. Use Relaxation Techniques:

- Deep Breathing: Practice deep breathing exercises to calm your mind and body before and during social interactions.

- Progressive Muscle Relaxation: Use progressive muscle relaxation techniques to release physical tension and promote relaxation.

- Visualization: Visualize yourself successfully navigating social situations. Imagine feeling calm and confident during interactions.

Everyday Anxiety

EVERYDAY ANXIETY CAN arise from various sources, such as daily responsibilities, unexpected challenges, or personal concerns. Here are some techniques for managing everyday anxiety:

1. Establish a Routine:

- Consistent Schedule: Create a consistent daily schedule to provide structure and predictability. A routine can help reduce uncertainty and anxiety.

- Balanced Lifestyle: Incorporate activities that promote well-being, such as exercise, healthy eating, adequate sleep, and relaxation techniques.

- Set Priorities: Focus on what is most important each day and prioritize tasks accordingly. This can help prevent feeling overwhelmed.

2. Practice Self-Care:

- Physical Self-Care: Engage in regular physical activity, eat nutritious meals, and get enough sleep. Taking care of your body can improve overall well-being and reduce anxiety.

- Emotional Self-Care: Allow yourself to express and process emotions through journaling, talking to a trusted friend, or seeking therapy. Emotional self-care can help you manage stress and anxiety.

- Mental Self-Care: Stimulate your mind with activities you enjoy, such as reading, puzzles, or learning new skills. Mental self-care can improve focus and reduce anxiety.

3. Use Coping Strategies:

- Deep Breathing: Practice deep breathing exercises to calm your mind and body during moments of anxiety.

- Mindfulness: Practice mindfulness to stay present and focused on the current moment. This can help reduce rumination and worry.

- Positive Affirmations: Use positive affirmations to counter negative thoughts and boost self-confidence. Repeat affirmations such as "I am capable" or "I can handle this."

4. Build a Support System:

- Connect with Others: Maintain connections with family, friends, and support groups. Social support can provide comfort and encouragement during challenging times.

- Seek Professional Help: If anxiety becomes overwhelming, consider seeking help from a therapist or counselor. Professional support can provide valuable tools and strategies for managing anxiety.

- Join Online Communities: Participate in online communities or forums related to anxiety management. Connecting with others who share similar experiences can provide a sense of belonging and support.

Creating an Anxiety Management Plan

AN ANXIETY MANAGEMENT plan is a personalized strategy that outlines specific steps and techniques for managing anxiety. Creating a plan can help you feel more in control and prepared to handle anxiety in various situations.

Steps to Create an Anxiety Management Plan

1. IDENTIFY TRIGGERS:

- Recognize Patterns: Pay attention to situations, thoughts, or events that trigger your anxiety. Identifying patterns can help you anticipate and prepare for potential anxiety-provoking situations.

- Write It Down: Keep a journal to document your anxiety triggers and how they affect you. Writing down your experiences can provide valuable insights and help you identify common themes.

2. Develop Coping Strategies:

- List Techniques: Create a list of coping strategies that work for you. Include techniques such as deep breathing, mindfulness, exercise, and positive affirmations.

- Practice Regularly: Practice your coping strategies regularly to build confidence and make them more effective during moments of anxiety.

- Personalize Your Plan: Tailor your coping strategies to your specific needs and preferences. Choose techniques that resonate with you and are practical for your lifestyle.

3. Set Goals:

- Short-Term Goals: Set achievable short-term goals for managing anxiety. For example, aim to use deep breathing exercises during stressful moments at work.

- Long-Term Goals: Set long-term goals for overall well-being and anxiety management. For example, aim to build a consistent exercise routine or develop healthier sleep habits.

4. Create a Support System:

- Identify Support People: List family members, friends, or colleagues who can provide support and encouragement. Reach out to them when you need assistance or a listening ear.

- Join Support Groups: Consider joining support groups or online communities related to anxiety management. Connecting with others who share similar experiences can provide valuable support and insights.

5. Monitor Progress:

- Track Your Progress: Keep track of your progress in managing anxiety. Document your successes, challenges, and any adjustments you make to your plan.

- Reflect Regularly: Reflect on your progress regularly to assess what is working and what may need improvement. Adjust your plan as needed to ensure it remains effective and relevant.

Using Technology and Apps to Support Anxiety Management

TECHNOLOGY AND APPS can be valuable tools for managing anxiety. They offer convenient access to resources, support, and techniques that can help reduce anxiety and improve well-being.

Popular Anxiety Management Apps

1. HEADSPACE:

- Features: Headspace offers guided meditation and mindfulness exercises designed to reduce stress and anxiety. The app includes a variety of sessions, such as breathing exercises, sleep stories, and focus-enhancing techniques.

- Benefits: Headspace can help individuals develop a regular meditation practice, improve mindfulness, and promote relaxation.

2. Calm:

- Features: Calm provides guided meditation, sleep stories, breathing exercises, and relaxation techniques. The app includes content designed to reduce anxiety, improve sleep, and enhance overall well-being.

- Benefits: Calm offers a user-friendly interface and a wide range of content that can be tailored to individual needs and preferences.

3. BetterHelp:

- Features: BetterHelp connects users with licensed therapists for online therapy sessions. The app allows for messaging, phone calls, and video sessions, providing flexible access to professional support.

- Benefits: BetterHelp offers convenient access to therapy, making it easier for individuals to seek professional help for anxiety management.

4. Sanvello:

- Features: Sanvello combines cognitive-behavioral therapy (CBT) techniques with mindfulness and mood tracking. The app includes guided journeys, tools for tracking mood and progress, and community support.

- Benefits: Sanvello provides a comprehensive approach to managing anxiety and offers personalized tools and resources.

5. MindShift:

- Features: MindShift focuses on helping individuals manage anxiety through evidence-based techniques. The app includes tools for relaxation, mindfulness, and cognitive-behavioral strategies, as well as tips for specific situations like social anxiety and panic attacks.

- Benefits: MindShift is designed to be practical and easy to use, offering immediate support and guidance for managing anxiety.

Benefits of Using Technology and Apps

1. ACCESSIBILITY:

- Convenient Access: Apps and technology provide convenient access to resources and support, making it easier to incorporate anxiety management into daily life.

- 24/7 Availability: Many apps offer support around the clock, allowing individuals to access tools and techniques whenever they need them.

2. Personalized Support:

- Tailored Content: Many apps offer personalized content based on individual needs and preferences. This can include customized meditation sessions, mood tracking, and goal-setting features.

- Progress Tracking: Apps often include features for tracking progress and monitoring changes in anxiety levels. This can help individuals identify patterns and assess the effectiveness of their strategies.

3. Variety of Tools:

- Diverse Techniques: Apps provide a wide range of tools and techniques for managing anxiety, including guided meditation, relaxation exercises, cognitive-behavioral strategies, and more.

- Multimedia Resources: Many apps include audio, video, and interactive content, making it easier to engage with and practice anxiety management techniques.

4. Community and Support:

- Online Communities: Some apps include features for connecting with online communities and support groups. This can provide additional support, encouragement, and shared experiences.

- Professional Guidance: Apps that offer access to licensed therapists or counselors can provide professional guidance and support for managing anxiety.

Real-Life Applications and Success Stories

TO ILLUSTRATE THE EFFECTIVENESS of coping strategies and technology for managing anxiety, here are real-life applications and success stories of individuals who have successfully managed their anxiety in daily life.

Case Study 1: Managing Work-Related Anxiety with Time Management and Technology

BACKGROUND: LISA IS a 32-year-old marketing manager who has been experiencing work-related anxiety due to a heavy workload and tight deadlines. Her anxiety often manifests as difficulty concentrating, restlessness, and physical tension.

Coping Strategies: Lisa implemented several time management techniques to manage her workload and reduce anxiety. She created a daily to-do list, prioritized tasks, and used the Pomodoro Technique to maintain focus and productivity. Lisa also personalized her workspace with calming colors and plants to create a more relaxing environment.

Technology and Apps: Lisa used the app Trello to organize her tasks and track progress. She also used the Calm app for guided meditation and relaxation exercises during breaks. The combination of time management techniques and technology helped Lisa stay organized, reduce stress, and improve her overall well-being.

Results: After implementing these strategies, Lisa noticed a significant reduction in her work-related anxiety. She felt more in control of her workload, experienced fewer physical symptoms of anxiety, and enjoyed a more balanced and productive workday.

Case Study 2: Overcoming Social Anxiety with Gradual Exposure and Mindfulness

BACKGROUND: JOHN IS a 28-year-old graphic designer who has been struggling with social anxiety. His symptoms included intense fear of social interactions, avoidance of social situations, and difficulty speaking in public.

Coping Strategies: John used gradual exposure techniques to manage his social anxiety. He started by attending small gatherings and gradually worked his way up to larger events. John also practiced mindfulness and deep breathing exercises to stay present and calm during social interactions.

Technology and Apps: John used the Headspace app for guided meditation and mindfulness exercises. He also used the MindShift app for cognitive-behavioral strategies and tips for managing social anxiety.

Results: With regular practice and the support of these apps, John became more comfortable in social situations. He successfully attended social events, engaged in conversations, and even gave a presentation at work. The combination of gradual exposure and mindfulness techniques helped John reduce his social anxiety and improve his confidence.

Case Study 3: Creating an Anxiety Management Plan and Using Online Therapy

BACKGROUND: SARAH IS a 35-year-old nurse who has been experiencing generalized anxiety disorder (GAD). Her symptoms included chronic worry, muscle tension, and difficulty sleeping.

Coping Strategies: Sarah created a personalized anxiety management plan that included identifying triggers, developing coping strategies, and setting goals. She practiced deep breathing, progressive muscle relaxation, and positive affirmations regularly.

Technology and Apps: Sarah used the BetterHelp app to connect with a licensed therapist for online therapy sessions. She also used the Sanvello app to track her mood, practice cognitive-behavioral techniques, and monitor her progress.

Results: After several months of implementing her anxiety management plan and participating in online therapy, Sarah experienced a significant reduction in her anxiety symptoms. She felt more in control of her thoughts and emotions, improved her sleep quality, and enjoyed a greater sense of well-being.

Conclusion

Managing anxiety in daily life requires a combination of practical coping strategies, personalized planning, and the use of technology and apps. Techniques such as time management, gradual exposure, mindfulness, and self-care can help individuals handle anxiety in various situations, whether at work, in social settings, or during everyday activities.

Creating an anxiety management plan involves identifying triggers, developing coping strategies, setting goals, and building a support system. Monitoring progress and making adjustments as needed can ensure the plan remains effective and relevant.

Technology and apps offer convenient and accessible tools for anxiety management. They provide personalized support, a variety of techniques, and community connections that can enhance overall well-being.

Real-life applications and success stories, such as those of Lisa, John, and Sarah, demonstrate the effectiveness of combining coping strategies and technology for managing anxiety. Their experiences highlight the positive impact of practical tips, personalized planning, and technological support on mental health and well-being.

Remember, managing anxiety is a journey that requires patience, persistence, and support. With the right knowledge, resources, and strategies, you can take control of your anxiety and work toward a future free from excessive fear and stress.

Chapter 12: Long-Term Strategies for Resilience

Building Emotional Resilience

Building emotional resilience is essential for long-term anxiety management and overall mental well-being. Resilience helps individuals adapt to stress, recover from setbacks, and maintain progress in their anxiety management journey. This chapter explores the importance of developing a growth mindset, strategies for maintaining progress and preventing relapse, and the significance of celebrating successes and learning from setbacks.

Developing a Growth Mindset

A GROWTH MINDSET, A concept popularized by psychologist Carol Dweck, is the belief that abilities and intelligence can be developed through dedication and hard work. This mindset fosters a love for learning and resilience essential for great accomplishments. Developing a growth mindset can be a powerful tool in building emotional resilience.

Characteristics of a Growth Mindset

1. EMBRACING CHALLENGES: Individuals with a growth mindset view challenges as opportunities for growth and learning rather than obstacles to be avoided. They understand that facing challenges can lead to personal development and resilience.

2. Persistence in the Face of Setbacks: A growth mindset encourages persistence and perseverance. Instead of giving up when faced with difficulties, individuals with a growth mindset continue to strive toward their goals, learning from setbacks along the way.

3. Effort as a Path to Mastery: People with a growth mindset believe that effort is crucial for improvement and mastery. They recognize that hard work and dedication can lead to success, regardless of initial talent or ability.

4. Learning from Criticism: Constructive criticism is seen as valuable feedback rather than a personal attack. Individuals with a growth mindset use criticism to identify areas for improvement and refine their skills.

5. Finding Inspiration in Others' Success: Instead of feeling threatened by others' success, individuals with a growth mindset find inspiration and learn from them. They believe that others' achievements can motivate and guide their own efforts.

Steps to Develop a Growth Mindset

1. SELF-REFLECTION: Reflect on your current mindset and beliefs about your abilities. Identify any fixed mindset thoughts, such as "I'm just not good at this" or "I can't change." Acknowledge these thoughts and challenge their validity.

2. Embrace Challenges: Actively seek out challenges and view them as opportunities for growth. When faced with a difficult task, remind yourself that it is an opportunity to learn and improve.

3. Focus on Effort: Recognize the value of effort in achieving your goals. Celebrate the hard work you put into tasks, regardless of the outcome. Understand that consistent effort leads to progress over time.

4. Learn from Criticism: View constructive criticism as valuable feedback that can help you grow. Instead of taking it personally, use it to identify areas for improvement and develop new strategies.

5. Cultivate Curiosity: Foster a love for learning and curiosity about the world. Explore new interests, take up new hobbies, and continue to seek knowledge and personal growth.

6. Surround Yourself with a Growth-Minded Community: Engage with individuals who have a growth mindset and support your journey. Surrounding yourself with positive influences can reinforce your own growth mindset.

Strategies for Maintaining Progress and Preventing Relapse

MAINTAINING PROGRESS and preventing relapse is crucial for long-term anxiety management. Developing sustainable strategies and habits can help individuals stay on track and continue to build resilience.

Establishing Healthy Habits

1. CONSISTENT ROUTINE: Establishing a consistent daily routine can provide structure and stability. A routine that includes healthy habits such as regular exercise, balanced nutrition, and adequate sleep can support overall well-being and reduce anxiety.

2. Mindfulness and Relaxation: Incorporate mindfulness and relaxation techniques into your daily routine. Practices such as meditation, deep breathing, and progressive muscle relaxation can help manage stress and promote emotional resilience.

3. Regular Physical Activity: Engaging in regular physical activity can reduce anxiety and improve mood. Choose activities that you enjoy and make them a regular part of your routine. Aim for at least 30 minutes of moderate exercise most days of the week.

4. Balanced Nutrition: A balanced diet rich in essential nutrients supports brain health and overall well-being. Focus on whole, unprocessed foods, and avoid excessive caffeine and sugar, which can exacerbate anxiety.

5. Adequate Sleep: Prioritize sleep by establishing a consistent sleep schedule and creating a relaxing bedtime routine. Adequate sleep is essential for mental and physical health and can help reduce anxiety.

Building a Support Network

1. CONNECT WITH LOVED Ones: Maintain strong connections with family and friends. Social support provides emotional comfort and practical assistance, which can help you navigate challenges and maintain progress.

2. Join Support Groups: Participate in support groups or online communities where you can share experiences and receive encouragement from others who understand what you're going through. Support groups can provide valuable insights and motivation.

3. Seek Professional Support: Continue to seek support from therapists or counselors, even after significant progress has been made. Regular therapy sessions can help you stay on track, address new challenges, and reinforce coping strategies.

Monitoring and Reflecting on Progress

1. TRACK YOUR PROGRESS: Keep a journal to document your journey, noting successes, challenges, and any changes in your anxiety levels. Tracking your progress can help you identify patterns and areas for improvement.

2. Set Realistic Goals: Set realistic and achievable goals for your anxiety management journey. Break larger goals into smaller, manageable steps and celebrate your achievements along the way.

3. Regular Reflection: Take time to reflect on your progress regularly. Assess what strategies are working well and identify any areas that need adjustment. Reflecting on your journey can provide valuable insights and reinforce your commitment to long-term resilience.

Developing Coping Strategies

1. IDENTIFY TRIGGERS: Continue to identify and understand your anxiety triggers. Awareness of triggers can help you anticipate and prepare for potential challenges.

2. Develop Coping Mechanisms: Build a toolkit of coping mechanisms that work for you. This may include relaxation techniques, cognitive-behavioral strategies, physical activity, and creative outlets.

3. Practice Self-Compassion: Treat yourself with kindness and understanding, especially during challenging times. Self-compassion can help you navigate setbacks with resilience and maintain a positive outlook.

Preventing Relapse

1. RECOGNIZE EARLY Warning Signs: Be aware of early warning signs of anxiety relapse, such as changes in mood, increased stress, or avoidance behaviors. Recognizing these signs early can help you take proactive steps to address them.

2. Stay Consistent with Treatment: Continue to follow your treatment plan, even when you feel better. Consistency with therapy, medication (if prescribed), and healthy habits can help prevent relapse.

3. Develop a Relapse Prevention Plan: Create a relapse prevention plan that outlines specific steps to take if you notice early warning signs. This plan may include reaching out to a therapist, using coping strategies, and seeking support from loved ones.

4. Practice Stress Management: Develop effective stress management techniques to handle life's challenges. This may include time management, setting boundaries, and practicing relaxation techniques.

Celebrating Successes and Learning from Setbacks

CELEBRATING SUCCESSES and learning from setbacks are essential components of building emotional resilience. Recognizing and appreciating your achievements can boost self-esteem and motivation, while learning from setbacks can provide valuable insights and opportunities for growth.

Celebrating Successes

1. ACKNOWLEDGE ACHIEVEMENTS: Take time to acknowledge and celebrate your achievements, no matter how small. Recognize the effort and progress you have made in managing your anxiety.

2. Reward Yourself: Reward yourself for reaching milestones and achieving goals. Choose meaningful rewards that bring you joy and reinforce positive behaviors.

3. Share Your Successes: Share your successes with loved ones or support groups. Celebrating with others can enhance your sense of accomplishment and strengthen your support network.

4. Reflect on Progress: Reflect on your journey and the progress you have made. Consider how far you have come and the skills you have developed along the way.

Learning from Setbacks

1. EMBRACE SETBACKS as Learning Opportunities: View setbacks as opportunities for growth and learning. Understand that setbacks are a normal part of the recovery process and do not define your overall progress.

2. Analyze Setbacks: Reflect on the circumstances and factors that contributed to the setback. Identify any patterns, triggers, or challenges that need to be addressed.

3. Adjust Strategies: Use the insights gained from setbacks to adjust your coping strategies and treatment plan. Consider what changes or improvements can be made to prevent similar setbacks in the future.

4. Practice Self-Compassion: Be kind and compassionate to yourself during setbacks. Avoid self-criticism and focus on the positive steps you can take to move forward.

Real-Life Applications and Success Stories

TO ILLUSTRATE THE EFFECTIVENESS of long-term strategies for resilience, here are real-life applications and success stories of individuals who have successfully built emotional resilience and maintained progress in their anxiety management journey.

Case Study 1: Developing a Growth Mindset and Building Resilience

BACKGROUND: EMILY IS a 30-year-old teacher who has been struggling with generalized anxiety disorder (GAD). Her symptoms included chronic worry, muscle tension, and difficulty concentrating.

Growth Mindset: Emily worked with a therapist to develop a growth mindset. She began to view challenges as opportunities for growth and focused on the effort she put into managing her anxiety. Emily embraced constructive criticism and used it to improve her coping strategies.

Resilience Building: Emily established a consistent routine that included regular exercise, mindfulness meditation, and balanced nutrition. She also maintained strong connections with her family and joined a support group for individuals with anxiety.

Results: Over time, Emily's growth mindset and resilience-building efforts led to significant improvements in her anxiety management. She felt more confident in her ability to handle stress and maintained progress even during challenging times. Emily's journey demonstrates the power of a growth mindset and resilience in long-term anxiety management.

Case Study 2: Maintaining Progress and Preventing Relapse

BACKGROUND: JOHN IS a 35-year-old software engineer who has been experiencing social anxiety disorder (SAD). His symptoms included intense fear of social interactions and avoidance of social situations.

Maintaining Progress: John developed a personalized anxiety management plan that included regular exposure to social situations, cognitive-behavioral strategies, and mindfulness practices. He tracked his progress in a journal and set realistic goals for his social interactions.

Preventing Relapse: John recognized early warning signs of anxiety relapse, such as increased avoidance behaviors and negative thoughts. He created a relapse prevention plan that included reaching out to his therapist, using relaxation techniques, and seeking support from friends.

Results: By maintaining consistent progress and using his relapse prevention plan, John was able to manage his social anxiety effectively. He successfully navigated social situations, built meaningful connections, and prevented relapse. John's journey highlights the importance of maintaining progress and having a proactive plan to prevent relapse.

Case Study 3: Celebrating Successes and Learning from Setbacks

BACKGROUND: SARAH IS a 40-year-old nurse who has been experiencing panic disorder. Her symptoms included recurrent panic attacks, rapid heart rate, and fear of losing control.

Celebrating Successes: Sarah made it a point to celebrate her successes, no matter how small. She acknowledged her achievements, such as successfully using coping strategies during a panic attack or completing a stressful task without experiencing anxiety. Sarah rewarded herself with activities she enjoyed, such as spending time in nature or treating herself to a favorite meal.

Learning from Setbacks: Sarah experienced occasional setbacks in her anxiety management journey. Instead of feeling discouraged, she embraced these setbacks as learning opportunities. She reflected on the factors that contributed to the setback, adjusted her coping strategies, and practiced self-compassion.

Results: By celebrating her successes and learning from setbacks, Sarah built emotional resilience and maintained progress in managing her panic disorder. She felt more confident in her ability to handle anxiety and continued to make positive strides in her recovery. Sarah's journey demonstrates the importance of recognizing achievements and using setbacks as opportunities for growth.

Conclusion

Building emotional resilience is essential for long-term anxiety management and overall mental well-being. Developing a growth mindset, maintaining progress, preventing relapse, and celebrating successes are key components of building resilience.

A growth mindset fosters a love for learning, persistence in the face of setbacks, and the belief that abilities can be developed through effort and dedication. Establishing healthy habits, building a support network, and regularly monitoring progress are crucial strategies for maintaining progress and preventing relapse.

Celebrating successes boosts self-esteem and motivation, while learning from setbacks provides valuable insights and opportunities for growth. Real-life applications and success stories, such as those of Emily, John, and Sarah, demonstrate the effectiveness of long-term strategies for resilience.

Remember, building emotional resilience is a journey that requires patience, persistence, and support. With the right knowledge, resources, and strategies, you can develop resilience and work toward a future free from excessive fear and stress.

Chapter 13: Helping Others with Anxiety and Phobias

Supporting Loved Ones

Anxiety and phobias can significantly impact the lives of those affected, as well as their loved ones. Understanding how to recognize the signs of anxiety and phobias, offering effective support, and accessing resources can make a significant difference in the lives of those dealing with these conditions. This chapter focuses on how to recognize anxiety and phobias in others, effective ways to offer support and encouragement, and valuable resources for families and caregivers.

How to Recognize Anxiety and Phobias in Others

RECOGNIZING ANXIETY and phobias in others is the first step toward providing support. Anxiety disorders and phobias can manifest in various ways, including emotional, behavioral, and physical symptoms. Being aware of these signs can help you identify when someone you care about may be struggling.

Emotional Symptoms

1. EXCESSIVE WORRY: One of the most common signs of anxiety is excessive worry or fear that is disproportionate to the situation. This worry can be persistent and difficult to control.

2. Irritability: Individuals with anxiety may become easily irritable or agitated, especially when dealing with stressors.

3. Feelings of Dread: People with anxiety often experience a sense of impending doom or dread, even when there is no immediate threat.

4. Restlessness: Anxiety can cause restlessness or an inability to relax. Individuals may feel constantly on edge or unable to sit still.

5. Panic Attacks: Panic attacks are sudden episodes of intense fear or discomfort, accompanied by physical symptoms such as a racing heart, sweating, and shortness of breath.

Behavioral Symptoms

1. AVOIDANCE: AVOIDING situations, places, or activities that trigger anxiety is a common behavioral symptom. This avoidance can interfere with daily life and responsibilities.

2. Social Withdrawal: People with social anxiety may withdraw from social interactions, isolate themselves, or avoid social situations altogether.

3. Compulsive Behaviors: Some individuals with anxiety engage in repetitive behaviors or rituals as a way to cope with their anxiety. These behaviors can be time-consuming and interfere with daily life.

4. Difficulty Concentrating: Anxiety can affect concentration and focus, making it challenging to complete tasks or stay engaged in activities.

5. Changes in Routine: Noticeable changes in daily routines, such as disrupted sleep patterns or changes in eating habits, can be signs of anxiety.

Physical Symptoms

1. MUSCLE TENSION: Chronic muscle tension, especially in the neck, shoulders, and back, is a common physical symptom of anxiety.

2. Headaches: Frequent headaches or migraines can be linked to anxiety and stress.

3. Stomach Issues: Gastrointestinal problems, such as stomachaches, nausea, and diarrhea, can be associated with anxiety.

4. Fatigue: Anxiety can cause persistent fatigue, even when the individual is getting enough sleep.

5. Shortness of Breath: Difficulty breathing, rapid breathing, or feeling like you can't catch your breath are common physical symptoms of anxiety.

Effective Ways to Offer Support and Encouragement

ONCE YOU HAVE RECOGNIZED the signs of anxiety and phobias in a loved one, the next step is to offer support and encouragement. Your approach can significantly impact their well-being and recovery. Here are some effective ways to support someone with anxiety and phobias:

Providing Emotional Support

1. LISTEN ACTIVELY: Offer a listening ear without judgment. Allow your loved one to express their feelings and thoughts without interruption. Show empathy and understanding.

2. Validate Their Feelings: Acknowledge their emotions and let them know that their feelings are valid. Avoid dismissing or minimizing their anxiety.

3. Encourage Open Communication: Create a safe space for open and honest communication. Encourage your loved one to share their experiences and concerns with you.

4. Be Patient: Recovery from anxiety and phobias takes time. Be patient and understanding, and avoid pressuring them to "get over it" quickly.

5. Reassure Them: Provide reassurance and comfort. Let them know that you are there for them and that they are not alone in their struggles.

Offering Practical Support

1. HELP WITH DAILY Tasks: Offer to help with daily tasks that may be overwhelming for them. This could include running errands, cooking meals, or assisting with household chores.

2. Accompany Them to Appointments: Offer to accompany them to therapy or medical appointments. Your presence can provide support and reduce their anxiety about seeking help.

3. Encourage Healthy Habits: Encourage healthy habits such as regular exercise, balanced nutrition, and adequate sleep. Offer to join them in these activities to provide motivation and support.

4. Assist with Coping Strategies: Help them develop and practice coping strategies. This could include mindfulness exercises, deep breathing techniques, or relaxation practices.

5. Respect Their Boundaries: Understand and respect their boundaries. Avoid pushing them into situations that may trigger their anxiety or phobias.

Encouraging Professional Help

1. EDUCATE YOURSELF: Learn about anxiety and phobias to better understand what your loved one is experiencing. This knowledge can help you provide informed support.

2. Normalize Seeking Help: Encourage your loved one to seek professional help by normalizing therapy and counseling. Let them know that seeking help is a sign of strength, not weakness.

3. Offer Resources: Provide information about mental health resources, such as therapists, support groups, and helplines. Offer to help them find a suitable professional.

4. Support Their Decisions: Support their decisions regarding treatment and respect their autonomy. Encourage them to take an active role in their recovery journey.

5. Be a Source of Encouragement: Offer encouragement and positive reinforcement throughout their treatment. Celebrate their progress and milestones, no matter how small.

Resources for Families and Caregivers

FAMILIES AND CAREGIVERS play a vital role in supporting individuals with anxiety and phobias. Accessing resources and support can help them navigate this challenging journey more effectively.

Educational Resources

1. BOOKS AND ARTICLES: There are numerous books and articles available that provide valuable information about anxiety and phobias. Some recommended books include "The Anxiety and Phobia Workbook" by Edmund J. Bourne and "The Anxiety Toolkit" by Alice Boyes.

2. Online Courses: Many online courses and webinars offer education on anxiety and phobias. Websites like Coursera, Udemy, and the Anxiety and Depression Association of America (ADAA) offer courses on mental health topics.

3. Websites and Blogs: Reputable websites and blogs provide valuable information and resources for families and caregivers. Some trusted sources include the National Institute of Mental Health (NIMH), the American Psychological Association (APA), and the Anxiety and Depression Association of America (ADAA).

Support Groups for Families and Caregivers

1. IN-PERSON SUPPORT Groups: Many communities offer in-person support groups for families and caregivers of individuals with anxiety and phobias. These groups provide a safe space to share experiences, seek advice, and receive emotional support.

2. Online Support Groups: Online support groups offer the convenience of connecting with others from the comfort of home. Websites like Mental Health America (MHA) and Health Unlocked host online communities for families and caregivers.

3. Social Media Groups: Platforms like Facebook have groups dedicated to supporting families and caregivers of individuals with anxiety and phobias. These groups provide a space for sharing experiences, asking questions, and offering support.

Professional Support for Families and Caregivers

1. FAMILY THERAPY: Family therapy involves working with a therapist to address family dynamics and improve communication. It can help families understand how to support their loved ones and address any conflicts or challenges.

2. Caregiver Counseling: Caregivers may benefit from individual counseling to address their own emotional needs and stress. Counseling can provide coping strategies and support for managing caregiver responsibilities.

3. Helplines and Hotlines: Many organizations offer helplines and hotlines for families and caregivers seeking support and information. The National Alliance on Mental Illness (NAMI) offers a helpline that provides information and support for families and caregivers.

Real-Life Applications and Success Stories

TO ILLUSTRATE THE EFFECTIVENESS of supporting loved ones with anxiety and phobias, here are real-life applications and success stories of individuals and families who have successfully navigated this journey.

Case Study 1: Supporting a Spouse with Social Anxiety

BACKGROUND: SARAH'S husband, John, has been struggling with social anxiety for several years. His symptoms included intense fear of social interactions, avoidance of social events, and difficulty speaking in public.

Recognizing the Signs: Sarah noticed that John became increasingly anxious and withdrawn before social events. He often made excuses to avoid gatherings and showed signs of distress when interacting with new people.

Providing Emotional Support: Sarah offered a listening ear and validated John's feelings without judgment. She encouraged open communication and reassured him that his feelings were valid.

Offering Practical Support: Sarah accompanied John to social events and stayed by his side to provide comfort. She also helped him develop and practice coping strategies, such as deep breathing exercises and positive affirmations.

Encouraging Professional Help: Sarah educated herself about social anxiety and encouraged John to seek professional help. She provided information about therapists and support groups and offered to help him find a suitable professional.

Results: With Sarah's support and encouragement, John began attending therapy and participating in social situations more comfortably. He developed effective coping strategies and gradually became more confident in social interactions. Sarah's understanding and support played a crucial role in John's progress.

Case Study 2: Supporting a Child with Specific Phobias

BACKGROUND: MARIA'S 10-year-old daughter, Lily, developed specific phobias, including a fear of dogs and thunderstorms. These phobias caused significant distress and impacted Lily's daily life.

Recognizing the Signs: Maria noticed that Lily exhibited extreme fear and avoidance behaviors when exposed to dogs or thunderstorms. She would become visibly anxious, cry, and refuse to go outside during storms.

Providing Emotional Support: Maria provided comfort and reassurance to Lily during moments of fear. She listened to Lily's concerns and validated her feelings, letting her know that it was okay to be afraid.

Offering Practical Support: Maria worked with Lily to gradually expose her to dogs in a controlled and safe manner. They started by looking at pictures of dogs, then progressed to watching videos and eventually visiting a friend's calm and friendly dog. Maria also created a calming routine for thunderstorms, including cozy blankets, favorite books, and relaxing music.

Encouraging Professional Help: Maria consulted with a child therapist who specialized in anxiety and phobias. The therapist provided guidance on exposure therapy and coping strategies for Lily.

Results: With Maria's support and the guidance of a therapist, Lily gradually overcame her fear of dogs and thunderstorms. She became more comfortable around dogs and developed coping strategies for managing her anxiety during storms. Maria's proactive approach and emotional support were instrumental in Lily's progress.

Case Study 3: Supporting a Friend with Generalized Anxiety Disorder

BACKGROUND: MARK'S friend, James, has been dealing with generalized anxiety disorder (GAD). His symptoms included chronic worry, muscle tension, and difficulty concentrating.

Recognizing the Signs: Mark noticed that James often expressed excessive worry about various aspects of life, including work, relationships, and health. James also showed signs of restlessness and physical tension.

Providing Emotional Support: Mark offered a listening ear and provided reassurance without judgment. He encouraged James to share his concerns and validated his feelings.

Offering Practical Support: Mark helped James develop a consistent routine that included regular exercise, mindfulness practices, and relaxation techniques. He also encouraged James to take breaks and prioritize self-care.

Encouraging Professional Help: Mark educated himself about GAD and encouraged James to seek professional help. He provided information about therapists and support groups and offered to accompany James to appointments if needed.

Results: With Mark's support and encouragement, James began attending therapy and implementing coping strategies for managing his anxiety. He developed a more balanced routine and experienced a reduction in his anxiety symptoms. Mark's understanding and proactive support played a crucial role in James's progress.

Conclusion

Supporting loved ones with anxiety and phobias requires understanding, patience, and proactive efforts. Recognizing the signs of anxiety and phobias, providing emotional and practical support, and encouraging professional help are essential components of effective support.

Families and caregivers can benefit from accessing educational resources, joining support groups, and seeking professional support to navigate this journey effectively. Real-life applications and success stories, such as those of Sarah, Maria, and Mark, demonstrate the positive impact of compassionate and informed support on the well-being and recovery of individuals with anxiety and phobias.

Remember, supporting someone with anxiety and phobias is a journey that requires empathy, dedication, and a willingness to learn. With the right knowledge, resources, and support, you can make a significant difference in the lives of your loved ones, helping them build resilience and work toward a future free from excessive fear and stress.

Chapter 14: Success Stories and Inspirational Journeys

Learning from Others

Inspiration can be drawn from the real-life stories of individuals who have faced anxiety and phobias head-on and emerged stronger. Their journeys, struggles, and triumphs provide valuable lessons and motivational takeaways for anyone dealing with similar challenges. This chapter delves into the real-life stories of individuals overcoming anxiety and phobias, features interviews and testimonials, and highlights the lessons learned and motivational insights from their experiences.

Real-Life Stories of Individuals Overcoming Anxiety and Phobias

Story 1: Overcoming Panic Disorder - Sarah's Journey

BACKGROUND: SARAH, a 32-year-old nurse, began experiencing panic attacks during her late twenties. Her panic attacks were characterized by sudden, intense episodes of fear, accompanied by physical symptoms such as rapid heart rate, shortness of breath, and dizziness. The unpredictability of the attacks caused Sarah to avoid many situations, fearing she would have another episode in public.

The Struggle: Sarah's panic attacks led to significant avoidance behaviors. She stopped going to crowded places, avoided driving, and withdrew from social activities. Her work as a nurse became increasingly challenging, as the fear of having a panic attack on the job added to her stress.

The Turning Point: Sarah decided to seek help after a particularly severe panic attack at work. She consulted with a therapist who specialized in cognitive-behavioral therapy (CBT). Through CBT, Sarah learned to identify and challenge the irrational thoughts that fueled her panic attacks. She also practiced exposure therapy, gradually facing situations she had been avoiding.

The Journey: Sarah's journey to recovery involved consistent effort and the support of her therapist, family, and friends. She began incorporating relaxation techniques such as deep breathing and progressive muscle relaxation into her daily routine. Sarah also joined a support group for individuals with panic disorder, where she found comfort and encouragement from others who understood her struggles.

The Triumph: Over time, Sarah gained control over her panic attacks. She no longer avoided situations out of fear and resumed activities she once enjoyed. Her confidence grew, and she even started mentoring others in her support group. Sarah's journey taught her the importance of persistence, self-compassion, and the power of seeking help.

Lessons Learned:

- Challenge Irrational Thoughts: Identifying and challenging irrational thoughts can significantly reduce the intensity of panic attacks.

- Gradual Exposure: Gradually facing feared situations through exposure therapy can help reduce avoidance behaviors and build confidence.

- Support Systems: Joining a support group and seeking help from loved ones and professionals can provide essential encouragement and guidance.

Story 2: Conquering Social Anxiety - Mark's Transformation

BACKGROUND: MARK, A 28-year-old graphic designer, had struggled with social anxiety since his teenage years. His fear of social interactions, particularly speaking in public or meeting new people, severely limited his personal and professional life. Mark often avoided social gatherings, networking events, and even speaking up in meetings at work.

The Struggle: Mark's social anxiety affected his self-esteem and career progression. Despite being talented in his field, he missed out on opportunities for advancement due to his fear of social interactions. His anxiety also took a toll on his personal relationships, as he found it challenging to form and maintain connections.

The Turning Point: The turning point for Mark came when he realized his social anxiety was holding him back from achieving his goals. Encouraged by a close friend, Mark sought help from a therapist who introduced him to cognitive-behavioral therapy (CBT). Through CBT, Mark learned to reframe negative thoughts about social situations and developed coping strategies for managing his anxiety.

The Journey: Mark's journey involved gradual exposure to social situations. He started small, attending local meetups and social gatherings with the support of his friend. Over time, he worked up to larger events and professional networking opportunities. Mark also practiced mindfulness and relaxation techniques to stay calm and focused during interactions.

The Triumph: Mark's transformation was remarkable. He became more confident in social settings, actively participated in work meetings, and even gave presentations. His career flourished as he took on leadership roles and expanded his professional network. Mark's personal relationships also improved, and he formed meaningful connections with new friends.

Lessons Learned:

- Reframe Negative Thoughts: Cognitive-behavioral techniques can help reframe negative thoughts and reduce social anxiety.

- Gradual Exposure: Slowly exposing oneself to social situations can build confidence and reduce fear.

- Mindfulness and Relaxation: Practicing mindfulness and relaxation techniques can help manage anxiety in real-time.

Story 3: Facing Specific Phobias - Emily's Success

BACKGROUND: EMILY, a 25-year-old college student, had a debilitating fear of heights (acrophobia) since childhood. Her phobia affected her ability to participate in everyday activities, such as taking flights, going to high floors in buildings, or even hiking with friends.

The Struggle: Emily's fear of heights limited her experiences and caused significant distress. She often felt embarrassed about her phobia and avoided discussing it with others. Her college life was impacted when she refused opportunities to study abroad or participate in certain field trips due to her fear.

The Turning Point: Emily's turning point came when she decided she no longer wanted her fear to control her life. She sought help from a psychologist who specialized in exposure therapy. With the psychologist's guidance, Emily developed an exposure hierarchy, starting with less anxiety-provoking situations and gradually working up to more challenging ones.

The Journey: Emily's exposure therapy involved a series of steps to gradually confront her fear. She began by looking at pictures of high places, then watching videos, and eventually visiting low-rise buildings. With each step, Emily used relaxation techniques to manage her anxiety and build resilience.

The Triumph: Emily's perseverance paid off. She successfully faced her fear of heights and participated in activities she once avoided. She took her first flight in years, enjoyed hiking with friends, and even visited an observation deck on a skyscraper. Emily's journey taught her the value of facing fears head-on and the strength she gained from each victory.

Lessons Learned:

- Exposure Therapy: Gradually confronting feared situations through exposure therapy can effectively reduce specific phobias.

- Relaxation Techniques: Incorporating relaxation techniques during exposure can help manage anxiety and build resilience.

- Persistence: Overcoming phobias requires consistent effort and persistence.

Interviews and Testimonials

TO GAIN DEEPER INSIGHTS into the experiences of individuals overcoming anxiety and phobias, we conducted interviews and gathered testimonials from people who have successfully managed these challenges. Their stories provide valuable perspectives and motivational takeaways.

Interview with James - Overcoming Generalized Anxiety Disorder

INTERVIEWER: THANK you for sharing your story, James. Can you tell us about your experience with generalized anxiety disorder (GAD)?

James: Absolutely. My experience with GAD began in my late twenties. I constantly worried about various aspects of my life, from work to personal relationships. The worry was overwhelming and affected my daily functioning. I often felt tense and had difficulty concentrating.

Interviewer: What steps did you take to manage your anxiety?

James: The first step was acknowledging that I needed help. I started seeing a therapist who specialized in cognitive-behavioral therapy (CBT). Through CBT, I learned to identify and challenge my negative thought patterns. I also practiced relaxation techniques like deep breathing and progressive muscle relaxation.

Interviewer: How did these strategies help you in your journey?

James: CBT was a game-changer for me. It helped me reframe my thoughts and approach situations with a more rational mindset. The relaxation techniques provided immediate relief during moments of intense anxiety. Over time, I noticed a significant reduction in my anxiety levels and felt more in control of my life.

Interviewer: What advice would you give to someone struggling with GAD?

James: My advice is to seek professional help and be open to trying different strategies. Recovery takes time, but with persistence and the right support, it's possible to manage anxiety effectively. Also, don't hesitate to lean on your support system—friends, family, and support groups can provide invaluable encouragement.

Testimonial from Lisa - Managing Panic Attacks

LISA'S STORY: MY PANIC attacks started in my early thirties, and they were terrifying. I felt like I was losing control, and the physical symptoms were overwhelming. It affected my work and personal life, as I constantly feared having another attack.

I decided to seek help and began working with a therapist who introduced me to exposure therapy and cognitive-behavioral strategies. The exposure therapy helped me face the situations I had been avoiding, and the cognitive-behavioral techniques taught me to challenge my irrational thoughts.

Over time, I regained control over my panic attacks. I no longer avoided activities out of fear and felt more confident in my ability to handle stress. The support from my therapist, family, and friends was crucial in my recovery. My journey taught me the importance of seeking help and the power of resilience.

Lessons Learned:

- Exposure Therapy: Gradually facing feared situations can reduce avoidance behaviors and build confidence.

- Cognitive-Behavioral Strategies: Challenging irrational thoughts can significantly reduce the intensity of panic attacks.

- Support Systems: Seeking help from professionals and loved ones is essential for recovery.

Lessons Learned and Motivational Takeaways

THE STORIES AND EXPERIENCES shared by individuals who have overcome anxiety and phobias offer valuable lessons and motivational takeaways. These insights can inspire and guide others on their journey to recovery.

Lesson 1: Seek Professional Help

SEEKING PROFESSIONAL help is a crucial step in managing anxiety and phobias. Therapists and counselors can provide evidence-based strategies, guidance, and support tailored to individual needs. Whether through cognitive-behavioral therapy, exposure therapy, or other therapeutic approaches, professional help can significantly impact the recovery process.

Motivational Takeaway: Don't hesitate to seek help. Professional support can provide the tools and strategies needed to manage anxiety and phobias effectively.

Lesson 2: Embrace Gradual Exposure

GRADUAL EXPOSURE TO feared situations is a powerful technique for overcoming anxiety and phobias. By taking small, manageable steps and gradually increasing the level of challenge, individuals can build confidence and reduce fear. Exposure therapy can be tailored to specific fears, allowing for a personalized approach to recovery.

Motivational Takeaway: Face your fears one step at a time. Gradual exposure can help you build resilience and regain control over your life.

Lesson 3: Practice Relaxation Techniques

RELAXATION TECHNIQUES such as deep breathing, mindfulness, and progressive muscle relaxation can provide immediate relief during moments of anxiety. These practices help calm the mind and body, reduce stress, and promote emotional resilience. Incorporating relaxation techniques into daily routines can support long-term anxiety management.

Motivational Takeaway: Incorporate relaxation techniques into your daily routine. These practices can help you stay calm and focused, even during challenging times.

Lesson 4: Build a Support System

HAVING A STRONG SUPPORT system is essential for managing anxiety and phobias. Friends, family, support groups, and online communities can provide encouragement, understanding, and practical assistance. Sharing experiences and seeking support from others who understand your struggles can significantly impact your recovery journey.

Motivational Takeaway: Surround yourself with supportive people. A strong support system can provide the encouragement and guidance needed to overcome anxiety and phobias.

Lesson 5: Practice Self-Compassion

SELF-COMPASSION INVOLVES treating yourself with kindness and understanding, especially during challenging times. It means recognizing that setbacks are a normal part of the recovery process and not being overly critical of yourself. Practicing self-compassion can help you navigate setbacks with resilience and maintain a positive outlook.

Motivational Takeaway: Be kind to yourself. Self-compassion can help you stay motivated and resilient on your journey to recovery.

Lesson 6: Celebrate Progress

CELEBRATING PROGRESS, no matter how small, is essential for maintaining motivation and building confidence. Acknowledging achievements and milestones reinforces positive behaviors and provides a sense of accomplishment. Celebrating progress can also remind you of how far you have come and inspire you to continue moving forward.

Motivational Takeaway: Celebrate your achievements. Recognizing and celebrating progress can boost your confidence and motivation.

Lesson 7: Stay Persistent

RECOVERY FROM ANXIETY and phobias is a journey that requires persistence and dedication. There may be setbacks along the way, but staying committed to your goals and continuing to practice coping strategies can lead to long-term success. Persistence involves maintaining a positive attitude and being willing to keep trying, even when faced with challenges.

Motivational Takeaway: Stay persistent. Your dedication and effort will lead to progress and success in managing anxiety and phobias.

Conclusion

The real-life stories, interviews, and testimonials shared in this chapter highlight the resilience and determination of individuals who have successfully managed anxiety and phobias. Their journeys provide valuable lessons and motivational takeaways that can inspire and guide others on their path to recovery.

Seeking professional help, embracing gradual exposure, practicing relaxation techniques, building a support system, practicing self-compassion, celebrating progress, and staying persistent are key components of effective anxiety management. These strategies can empower individuals to overcome their fears, build resilience, and achieve long-term well-being.

Remember, you are not alone on this journey. Learning from the experiences of others and applying these lessons can help you navigate your own path to recovery. With the right knowledge, resources, and support, you can overcome anxiety and phobias and work toward a future free from excessive fear and stress.

Chapter 15: Resources and Further Reading

Continuing Your Journey

Managing anxiety and phobias is an ongoing journey that requires access to reliable resources, support systems, and continuous learning. This chapter provides a comprehensive guide to recommended books, websites, organizations, online courses, workshops, and tools for ongoing self-improvement and support. These resources can help you deepen your understanding, develop new skills, and maintain progress in your anxiety management journey.

Recommended Books

BOOKS CAN BE A VALUABLE source of information, inspiration, and practical strategies for managing anxiety and phobias. Here are some highly recommended books that cover various aspects of anxiety management, from cognitive-behavioral techniques to mindfulness practices.

Cognitive-Behavioral Therapy (CBT) and Practical Guides

1. "THE ANXIETY AND Phobia Workbook" by Edmund J. Bourne

- This comprehensive workbook offers practical exercises and techniques for managing anxiety and phobias. It covers cognitive-behavioral strategies, relaxation techniques, and lifestyle changes. The workbook format allows readers to actively engage with the material and track their progress.

2. "Feeling Good: The New Mood Therapy" by David D. Burns

- This classic book on cognitive-behavioral therapy (CBT) provides evidence-based techniques for overcoming depression and anxiety. Dr. Burns explains how to identify and challenge negative thought patterns and develop healthier ways of thinking.

3. "The Anxiety Toolkit: Strategies for Fine-Tuning Your Mind and Moving Past Your Stuck Points" by Alice Boyes

- Dr. Alice Boyes offers practical strategies for managing anxiety in everyday life. The book includes tools for identifying anxiety triggers, challenging negative thoughts, and developing coping skills.

4. "When Panic Attacks: The New, Drug-Free Anxiety Therapy That Can Change Your Life" by David D. Burns

- This book focuses on CBT techniques for managing panic attacks and generalized anxiety. Dr. Burns provides practical exercises and case studies to illustrate how these techniques can be applied.

Mindfulness and Relaxation

1. "THE MIRACLE OF Mindfulness: An Introduction to the Practice of Meditation" by Thich Nhat Hanh

- Thich Nhat Hanh, a renowned Zen master, offers an introduction to mindfulness meditation. The book includes practical exercises for cultivating mindfulness and living in the present moment.

2. "Wherever You Go, There You Are: Mindfulness Meditation in Everyday Life" by Jon Kabat-Zinn

- Dr. Jon Kabat-Zinn, the founder of Mindfulness-Based Stress Reduction (MBSR), provides insights into mindfulness meditation and its applications in daily life. The book includes practical guidance for incorporating mindfulness into everyday activities.

3. "Full Catastrophe Living: Using the Wisdom of Your Body and Mind to Face Stress, Pain, and Illness" by Jon Kabat-Zinn

- This comprehensive guide to MBSR offers techniques for managing stress, pain, and anxiety through mindfulness meditation. Dr. Kabat-Zinn explains how to use mindfulness to improve overall well-being.

4. "Calm: Calm the Mind. Change the World" by Michael Acton Smith

- This book offers a variety of mindfulness exercises and relaxation techniques to help readers reduce stress and anxiety. It includes practical tips for incorporating mindfulness into daily life.

Specific Phobias and Social Anxiety

1. "OVERCOMING SOCIAL Anxiety and Shyness: A Self-Help Guide Using Cognitive Behavioral Techniques" by Gillian Butler

- Dr. Gillian Butler provides a self-help guide for managing social anxiety and shyness using CBT techniques. The book includes practical exercises and case studies to help readers develop confidence in social situations.

2. "The Shyness and Social Anxiety Workbook: Proven, Step-by-Step Techniques for Overcoming Your Fear" by Martin M. Antony and Richard P. Swinson

- This workbook offers evidence-based techniques for managing social anxiety and shyness. It includes practical exercises, worksheets, and strategies for building social confidence.

3. "The Phobia Workbook: Great Treatment Tips, Ways to Find Relief, and Much More!" by Martin M. Antony and Michelle G. Craske

- This workbook provides practical strategies for managing specific phobias using CBT and exposure therapy techniques. It includes step-by-step exercises and case studies.

Recommended Websites and Organizations

SEVERAL WEBSITES AND organizations provide valuable information, resources, and support for managing anxiety and phobias. These resources can help you stay informed, connect with others, and access professional guidance.

Mental Health Organizations

1. ANXIETY AND DEPRESSION Association of America (ADAA)

- Website: www.adaa.org

- The ADAA provides information on anxiety disorders, treatment options, and self-help strategies. The website includes articles, webinars, and a directory of mental health professionals.

2. National Institute of Mental Health (NIMH)

- Website: www.nimh.nih.gov

- The NIMH offers research-based information on mental health disorders, including anxiety and phobias. The website includes educational materials, news updates, and resources for finding help.

3. Mental Health America (MHA)

- Website: www.mhanational.org

- MHA provides resources for mental health education, advocacy, and support. The website includes screening tools, informational articles, and links to support services.

4. National Alliance on Mental Illness (NAMI)

- Website: www.nami.org

- NAMI offers support and education for individuals affected by mental illness. The website includes information on anxiety disorders, support groups, and advocacy initiatives.

Online Support Communities

1. 7 CUPS

- Website: www.7cups.com

- 7 Cups provides online emotional support through trained listeners and peer support communities. The website offers chat sessions, self-help guides, and community forums.

2. HealthUnlocked

- Website: www.healthunlocked.com

- HealthUnlocked hosts online communities for various health conditions, including anxiety and phobias. The platform allows users to connect with others, share experiences, and access support.

3. Reddit - Anxiety Community

- Website: www.reddit.com/r/anxiety

- The Anxiety subreddit is an active online community where individuals can share their experiences, seek advice, and offer support. The community is moderated to ensure a safe and supportive environment.

Online Courses and Workshops

ONLINE COURSES AND workshops offer opportunities for learning and skill-building from the comfort of your home. These programs cover various aspects of anxiety management, including CBT, mindfulness, and relaxation techniques.

Cognitive-Behavioral Therapy (CBT) Courses

1. CBT FOR ANXIETY and Depression - Beck Institute

- Website: www.beckinstitute.org

- The Beck Institute offers online courses on CBT for anxiety and depression. These courses provide evidence-based techniques and practical applications for managing anxiety.

2. Introduction to CBT - Udemy

- Website: www.udemy.com

- Udemy offers a range of online courses on CBT, including an introduction to CBT techniques for managing anxiety and depression. The courses are self-paced and include video lectures and practical exercises.

3. CBT for Social Anxiety - Coursera

- Website: www.coursera.org

- Coursera offers courses on CBT for social anxiety, developed by universities and mental health professionals. These courses provide insights into CBT strategies and practical tools for managing social anxiety.

Mindfulness and Relaxation Courses

1. MINDFULNESS-BASED Stress Reduction (MBSR) - Palouse Mindfulness

- Website: www.palousemindfulness.com

- Palouse Mindfulness offers a free, online MBSR course based on the program developed by Jon Kabat-Zinn. The course includes guided meditations, instructional videos, and practice exercises.

2. The Science of Well-Being - Coursera

- Website: www.coursera.org

- This popular course, offered by Yale University, covers topics related to well-being and happiness, including mindfulness and stress reduction techniques. The course is self-paced and includes video lectures and practical exercises.

3. Mindfulness for Anxiety and Stress - Mindful Schools

- Website: www.mindfulschools.org

- Mindful Schools offers online courses on mindfulness practices for managing anxiety and stress. The courses include guided meditations, instructional videos, and practical tips for incorporating mindfulness into daily life.

Workshops and Webinars

1. ANXIETY AND DEPRESSION Association of America (ADAA) Webinars

- Website: www.adaa.org

- The ADAA hosts webinars on various topics related to anxiety and depression. These webinars feature expert speakers and provide valuable information and practical strategies for managing anxiety.

2. Mental Health America (MHA) Workshops

- Website: www.mhanational.org

- MHA offers online workshops and webinars on mental health topics, including anxiety and stress management. The workshops provide practical tools and insights from mental health professionals.

3. NAMI Educational Programs

- Website: www.nami.org

- NAMI offers a range of educational programs and workshops for individuals affected by mental illness. These programs include courses on anxiety management, coping strategies, and self-care practices.

Tools for Ongoing Self-Improvement and Support

ONGOING SELF-IMPROVEMENT and support are essential for maintaining progress in anxiety management. Various tools, including mobile apps, journals, and self-help programs, can provide continuous support and encouragement.

Mobile Apps

1. HEADSPACE

- Website: www.headspace.com

- Headspace offers guided meditation and mindfulness exercises designed to reduce anxiety and stress. The app includes a variety of sessions, such as breathing exercises, sleep stories, and focus-enhancing techniques.

2. Calm

- Website: www.calm.com

- Calm provides guided meditation, sleep stories, breathing exercises, and relaxation techniques. The app includes content designed to reduce anxiety, improve sleep, and enhance overall well-being.

3. Sanvello

- Website: www.sanvello.com

- Sanvello combines CBT techniques with mindfulness and mood tracking. The app includes guided journeys, tools for tracking mood and progress, and community support.

4. MindShift

- Website: www.anxietycanada.com

- MindShift focuses on helping individuals manage anxiety through evidence-based techniques. The app includes tools for relaxation, mindfulness, and cognitive-behavioral strategies, as well as tips for specific situations like social anxiety and panic attacks.

Journals and Workbooks

1. THE ANXIETY JOURNAL: Exercises to Soothe Stress and Eliminate Anxiety Wherever You Are by Corinne Sweet

- This guided journal includes exercises and prompts designed to help individuals manage anxiety. It provides space for reflection, goal-setting, and tracking progress.

2. The Cognitive Behavioral Therapy Workbook for Anxiety: A Step-By-Step Program by William J. Knaus and Jon Carlson

- This workbook offers a structured program for managing anxiety using CBT techniques. It includes practical exercises, worksheets, and case studies.

3. The Mindfulness Journal: Daily Practices, Writing Prompts, and Reflections for Living in the Present Moment by Barrie Davenport

- This journal provides daily prompts and exercises for cultivating mindfulness and reducing anxiety. It includes space for reflection and goal-setting.

Self-Help Programs

1. THE FEAR FIGHTER Program

- Website: www.fearfighter.com

- Fear Fighter is an online CBT program designed to help individuals manage anxiety and phobias. The program includes interactive modules, exercises, and support from trained professionals.

2. MoodGYM

- Website: www.moodgym.com.au

- MoodGYM is an interactive, online program based on CBT principles. It offers modules for managing anxiety, depression, and stress, with exercises and feedback to track progress.

3. Living Life to the Full

- Website: www.llttf.com

- Living Life to the Full provides free online courses based on CBT techniques. The courses cover topics such as anxiety management, stress reduction, and building resilience.

Real-Life Applications and Success Stories

TO ILLUSTRATE THE EFFECTIVENESS of these resources and tools, here are real-life applications and success stories of individuals who have successfully used them to manage their anxiety and phobias.

Case Study 1: Using Mobile Apps for Daily Support

BACKGROUND: EMMA, A 29-year-old marketing executive, struggled with generalized anxiety disorder (GAD). She often felt overwhelmed by work stress and had difficulty managing her anxiety.

Resources Used: Emma started using the Calm app for guided meditation and relaxation exercises. She also used the Sanvello app to track her mood and practice CBT techniques.

Results: The daily meditation sessions from the Calm app helped Emma feel more relaxed and focused. The mood tracking and CBT exercises in the Sanvello app provided her with practical tools for managing anxiety. Emma experienced a significant reduction in her anxiety levels and felt more in control of her stress.

Case Study 2: Incorporating Mindfulness Practices

BACKGROUND: JAMES, a 35-year-old teacher, experienced social anxiety that affected his interactions with colleagues and students. He sought ways to build confidence and reduce anxiety in social situations.

Resources Used: James read "Wherever You Go, There You Are" by Jon Kabat-Zinn and began practicing mindfulness meditation. He also attended an online MBSR course through Palouse Mindfulness.

Results: The mindfulness practices helped James stay present and calm during social interactions. The MBSR course provided him with a structured approach to mindfulness and stress reduction. James noticed a significant improvement in his social anxiety and felt more confident in his interactions.

Case Study 3: Utilizing Online Support Communities

BACKGROUND: SARAH, a 42-year-old accountant, developed a specific phobia of flying after a turbulent flight experience. Her fear prevented her from traveling and affected her personal and professional life.

Resources Used: Sarah joined the Anxiety and Depression Association of America's (ADAA) online support community and participated in discussions about specific phobias. She also used the Fear Fighter program to practice exposure therapy.

Results: The online support community provided Sarah with encouragement and practical tips from others who had similar fears. The Fear Fighter program helped her gradually confront her fear of flying through exposure exercises. Sarah successfully took a short flight and felt more confident in her ability to manage her phobia.

Conclusion

Continuing your journey in managing anxiety and phobias requires access to reliable resources, support systems, and continuous learning. Recommended books, websites, organizations, online courses, workshops, and tools can provide valuable information, practical strategies, and ongoing support.

Whether through reading insightful books, participating in online courses, joining support communities, or using mobile apps, these resources can empower you to deepen your understanding, develop new skills, and maintain progress in your anxiety management journey.

Real-life applications and success stories demonstrate the effectiveness of these resources and tools. By incorporating these recommendations into your routine, you can build resilience, reduce anxiety, and work toward a future free from excessive fear and stress.

Remember, managing anxiety and phobias is an ongoing process that requires dedication, persistence, and support. With the right resources and a commitment to self-improvement, you can achieve long-term well-being and a fulfilling life.

Conclusion

Final Thoughts and Encouragement

AS WE COME TO THE CONCLUSION of this journey through understanding and managing anxiety and phobias, it is essential to recap the key points and strategies covered in this book. By revisiting these crucial elements, we can solidify our understanding and continue to strive for improvement. Additionally, we will emphasize the importance of persistence and self-compassion in the ongoing journey toward mental well-being.

Recap of Key Points and Strategies

Understanding Anxiety and Phobias

1. DEFINITION AND DIFFERENCES: Anxiety is a general term for various disorders that cause nervousness, fear, apprehension, and worrying. Phobias are intense, irrational fears of specific objects, activities, or situations. Understanding the distinction between the two helps in identifying and addressing the issues effectively.

2. Biological and Psychological Explanations: Anxiety can arise from a combination of genetic, biological, environmental, and psychological factors. The brain's chemistry, particularly involving neurotransmitters like serotonin and dopamine, plays a significant role in anxiety disorders.

3. Common Symptoms: Anxiety symptoms can be emotional (e.g., excessive worry, irritability), behavioral (e.g., avoidance of feared situations), and physical (e.g., muscle tension, headaches). Recognizing these symptoms is crucial for early intervention.

Recognizing and Diagnosing

1. IDENTIFYING TRIGGERS: Understanding what triggers anxiety or phobias helps in developing effective coping strategies. Common triggers include stress, trauma, certain medical conditions, and substance use.

2. Self-Assessment and Professional Help: Using self-assessment tools and questionnaires can provide insights into the severity of anxiety. Seeking professional help for a thorough diagnosis and personalized treatment plan is often necessary for managing anxiety effectively.

3. Understanding Diagnosis: A clear diagnosis helps in tailoring the treatment plan to address specific needs. Anxiety disorders include generalized anxiety disorder (GAD), panic disorder, social anxiety disorder, and specific phobias.

Effective Strategies for Managing Anxiety

1. COGNITIVE-BEHAVIORAL Techniques: Cognitive-behavioral therapy (CBT) is an evidence-based approach that helps individuals identify and challenge negative thought patterns. Practical exercises for challenging negative thoughts and real-life applications demonstrate the effectiveness of CBT.

2. Exposure Therapy: Gradually facing fears through exposure therapy can help reduce avoidance behaviors and build resilience. Creating an exposure hierarchy and practicing exposure exercises are key components of this approach.

3. Mindfulness and Relaxation Techniques: Mindfulness practices, such as meditation, breathing exercises, and progressive muscle relaxation, promote relaxation and reduce anxiety. Incorporating mindfulness into daily life can enhance overall well-being.

4. Lifestyle Changes: Building a healthier routine through regular exercise, balanced nutrition, adequate sleep, and self-care practices supports anxiety management. Establishing healthy habits and creating a balanced lifestyle are fundamental for long-term well-being.

5. Support Systems: Building a support network, including family, friends, support groups, and professional therapists, provides emotional and practical support. Sharing experiences and seeking help from others can significantly impact recovery.

6. Medication and Alternative Therapies: Medications, such as SSRIs, SNRIs, benzodiazepines, and beta-blockers, can be effective in managing anxiety. Alternative therapies, including acupuncture, herbal remedies, and aromatherapy, offer additional support.

Long-Term Strategies for Resilience

1. DEVELOPING A GROWTH Mindset: Embracing challenges, learning from setbacks, and viewing effort as a path to mastery are characteristics of a growth mindset. This mindset fosters resilience and a love for learning.

2. Maintaining Progress and Preventing Relapse: Establishing healthy habits, building a support network, and regularly monitoring progress are crucial for maintaining progress. Recognizing early warning signs and having a relapse prevention plan in place can prevent setbacks.

3. Celebrating Successes and Learning from Setbacks: Acknowledging achievements, rewarding progress, and reflecting on lessons learned from setbacks reinforce positive behaviors and build resilience. Practicing self-compassion is essential during challenging times.

Encouragement to Keep Striving for Improvement

MANAGING ANXIETY AND phobias is an ongoing journey that requires dedication, persistence, and continuous effort. It is important to remember that progress may not always be linear, and setbacks are a normal part of the process. However, with the right strategies and support, significant improvements are possible.

1. Stay Committed: Staying committed to your treatment plan, whether it involves therapy, medication, lifestyle changes, or a combination of these, is

essential for long-term success. Consistency is key to maintaining progress and achieving your goals.

2. Seek Support: Do not hesitate to seek support from friends, family, support groups, and mental health professionals. Building a strong support network can provide the encouragement and guidance needed to navigate challenges.

3. Embrace Growth and Learning: Continue to embrace a growth mindset and view each challenge as an opportunity for growth. Learning new skills, exploring different strategies, and being open to change can enhance your resilience.

4. Celebrate Small Wins: Acknowledge and celebrate your achievements, no matter how small. Each step forward is a testament to your strength and determination. Celebrating progress reinforces positive behaviors and boosts motivation.

5. Be Patient with Yourself: Recovery is a journey that takes time. Be patient with yourself and recognize that setbacks do not define your overall progress. Treat yourself with kindness and understanding, especially during difficult times.

Emphasizing the Importance of Persistence and Self-Compassion

PERSISTENCE AND SELF-compassion are fundamental components of the journey to managing anxiety and phobias. These qualities help individuals navigate the ups and downs of recovery and maintain a positive outlook.

The Role of Persistence

1. CONSISTENCY: PERSISTENCE involves consistently practicing the strategies and techniques that support your mental well-being. Whether it's attending therapy sessions, practicing mindfulness, or following a healthy routine, staying consistent is crucial.

2. Overcoming Setbacks: Setbacks are a natural part of the recovery process. Persistence means not giving up when faced with challenges and continuing to move forward. Each setback provides an opportunity to learn and grow.

3. Long-Term Commitment: Managing anxiety and phobias requires a long-term commitment. Persistence ensures that you stay focused on your goals and continue to work towards improvement, even when progress seems slow.

The Role of Self-Compassion

1. KINDNESS TO YOURSELF: Self-compassion involves treating yourself with the same kindness and understanding that you would offer a friend. Acknowledge your efforts and recognize that you are doing your best.

2. Understanding Human Imperfection: Understand that everyone experiences difficulties and setbacks. Being compassionate towards yourself means accepting your imperfections and recognizing that struggles are a part of the human experience.

3. Encouraging Self-Support: Self-compassion encourages you to support yourself through challenges rather than being self-critical. It involves using positive self-talk, practicing self-care, and seeking help when needed.

Real-Life Applications and Success Stories

TO ILLUSTRATE THE POWER of persistence and self-compassion, here are some real-life success stories of individuals who have successfully managed their anxiety and phobias through these principles.

Case Study 1: Persistence in Overcoming Generalized Anxiety Disorder

BACKGROUND: EMMA, A 35-year-old graphic designer, struggled with generalized anxiety disorder (GAD) for many years. Her anxiety manifested as chronic worry, restlessness, and difficulty concentrating.

Persistence: Emma committed to a comprehensive treatment plan that included CBT, medication, and lifestyle changes. She consistently attended therapy sessions, practiced mindfulness exercises, and maintained a healthy routine.

Self-Compassion: Throughout her journey, Emma practiced self-compassion by acknowledging her efforts and being kind to herself during setbacks. She recognized that recovery was a gradual process and celebrated her progress along the way.

Results: Over time, Emma experienced a significant reduction in her anxiety symptoms. Her persistence and self-compassion helped her build resilience and achieve long-term well-being. She now uses her experience to support others facing similar challenges.

Case Study 2: Self-Compassion in Managing Social Anxiety

BACKGROUND: JAMES, a 28-year-old teacher, experienced severe social anxiety that affected his interactions with colleagues and students. He often avoided social situations and struggled with self-esteem.

Persistence: James sought help from a therapist and began practicing CBT techniques to challenge his negative thoughts. He also gradually exposed himself to social situations, starting with small gatherings and working up to larger events.

Self-Compassion: James practiced self-compassion by accepting his imperfections and treating himself with kindness. He acknowledged his progress and learned to forgive himself for setbacks.

Results: James's persistence and self-compassion led to significant improvements in his social anxiety. He became more confident in social interactions and developed a positive self-image. James's journey demonstrates the power of self-compassion in overcoming anxiety.

Case Study 3: Combining Persistence and Self-Compassion in Facing Specific Phobias

BACKGROUND: SARAH, a 40-year-old nurse, developed a severe phobia of heights after a traumatic experience. Her phobia affected her ability to travel and participate in everyday activities.

Persistence: Sarah committed to exposure therapy, gradually confronting her fear of heights. She practiced relaxation techniques and maintained a consistent routine to support her progress.

Self-Compassion: Throughout her journey, Sarah practiced self-compassion by acknowledging her efforts and being patient with herself. She celebrated each step forward and used positive self-talk to overcome setbacks.

Results: Sarah's persistence and self-compassion helped her overcome her fear of heights. She successfully participated in activities she once avoided and regained her confidence. Sarah's story highlights the importance of combining persistence and self-compassion in managing phobias.

Conclusion: Final Thoughts and Encouragement

AS WE CONCLUDE THIS book, it is important to remember that managing anxiety and phobias is an ongoing journey that requires dedication, persistence, and self-compassion. The strategies and insights shared throughout this book provide a foundation for understanding and managing anxiety effectively.

1. Empower Yourself with Knowledge: Continue to educate yourself about anxiety and phobias. Knowledge empowers you to make informed decisions and take control of your mental well-being.

2. Implement Effective Strategies: Use the strategies and techniques discussed in this book to manage your anxiety. Whether it's CBT, exposure therapy, mindfulness practices, or lifestyle changes, find what works best for you and incorporate it into your daily routine.

3. Seek Support: Build a strong support network of friends, family, support groups, and mental health professionals. Sharing your journey with others and seeking help when needed can make a significant difference.

4. Practice Persistence and Self-Compassion: Stay committed to your goals and be patient with yourself. Recognize that setbacks are a natural part of the process and treat yourself with kindness and understanding.

5. Celebrate Your Progress: Acknowledge and celebrate your achievements, no matter how small. Each step forward is a testament to your strength and determination.

Remember, you are not alone on this journey. Many others have successfully managed their anxiety and phobias and have gone on to lead fulfilling lives. With the right knowledge, resources, and support, you too can overcome anxiety and phobias and work toward a future free from excessive fear and stress.

Stay committed, be kind to yourself, and keep striving for improvement. Your journey to mental well-being is unique, and every step you take brings you closer to a healthier, happier life.

Don't miss out!

Visit the website below and you can sign up to receive emails whenever Timothy Scott Phillips publishes a new book. There's no charge and no obligation.

https://books2read.com/r/B-A-KCQWC-YJMJF

BOOKS2READ

Connecting independent readers to independent writers.

About the Author

Timothy Scott Phillips is a dedicated author specializing in non-fiction self-help books that empower readers to overcome challenges and embrace personal growth. With a passion for mental health, resilience, and self-improvement, Timothy combines research-based insights with practical strategies to inspire lasting change. His work reflects a deep commitment to helping individuals navigate life's complexities, build confidence, and unlock their full potential. When he's not writing, Timothy enjoys mentoring, exploring nature, and connecting with his readers to share stories of transformation and hope. His books are a testament to the power of perseverance and the human spirit.